Black Pebble River
L.Y. 959
NEPUMUK
ENTROPIA
ENTROPIA
OBSIDIAN
BROTHERHOOD
ENTROPIA
LUNAR YEAR 1010
OCEANIC PEACE AGREEMENT
ENTROPIA
GRANDMOTHER OF THE SEA
The Great Solar Eclipse
L.Y. 999
KUKURSK
L.Y. 1012
AQUARAIL
ENTROPIA
GOVERNMENTAL HOPE WHISPERER
L.Y. 956
MARQUIS DE SALADE
ENTROPIA
ENTROPIA
BLUE STRIPED ARTWARE NATIONAL ANIMAL
ENTROPIA
XIII
THE WORLD OF PERPETUAL DREAMING
L.Y. 966
SOMNABUL
CITY OF SLEEPWALKERS
SUBNAUTICAL FLEET
ENTROPIA
HUNTERS OF THE DEEP
ENTROPIA
FIREFISH OF TAKASHIRO
SKY SAILOR GUILD since L.Y. 655
ENTROPIA
LUNAR YEAR 963
TRAVEL PETS AWARENESS
THE INDEPENDENT WHALE CITIES OF THE DEEP
L.Y. 1055
FUNGUS SANCTUARY
ENTROPIA
ENTROPIA
THE TREE SPIRITS OF KUKURSK
ENTROPIA'S WILD ROSE
ENTROPIA
BY AIRSHIP

AF823247

ENTROPIA

A COLLECTION OF UNUSUALLY RARE STAMPS

by
Christian Lorenz Scheurer

www.radioentropia.com

www.christianlorenzscheurer.com

Art Direction: Christian L. Scheurer
Layout Production: Marsha Stevenson
Copy Editing: Anna Skinner

Published by Design Studio Press
8577 Higuera Street
Culver City, CA 90232
Web site: www.designstudiopress.com
E-mail: info@designstudiopress.com

Printed in China
First Edition, November 2005
ISBN: 1-933492-04-X
Library of Congress Control Number:
2005933507

for my darling wife, laura

CHRISTIAN LORENZ SCHEURER was born in Bern, Switzerland. As the son of a zoologist father and an artist mother, he lived in many countries throughout his childhood, from the bush in South Africa to the Seychelle Islands. After winning the prestigious Philip Morris Award for his graphic novels and working on movies and award-winning commercials in Europe, Scheurer was struck by lightning. He then decided to pursue a career in Hollywood as a concept artist. During his U.S. career, Scheurer has worked on some of the most innovative movies, games, and commercials in the entertainment industry as a conceptual designer, matte painter, and art director.

CHRISTIAN LORENZ SCHEURER

Dear Interplanetary Philatelist and Stamp Enthusiast,

I am proud to share with you another highlight in my philatelic career: Entropia: A Collection of Unusually Rare Stamps. For you to understand the unique nature of this stamp collection, I would like to give you some information regarding Entropia and its philatelic history.

The word Entropia applies to the planet, the continent, and the nation state. As most serious interplanetary philatelists already know, Entropia is one of a few planets in the "Great Cosmic Disorder" that has produced memorable stamps of superior quality. (There have been attempts to produce stamps in the lunar system of Brandenburg 5 and on a couple of other obscure planets, but most of the stamps were destroyed in the great Supernova of lunar year -2201.) Therefore, in this publication I will solely focus on a collection of unusually rare stamps that have originated from the Royal Republic and later from the Direct Democracy of Entropia during the last 258 lunar years.

The map and charts will provide the rudimentary geographic and historical knowledge necessary to understand the following collection.

Sincerely yours,

P.S. If you are in possession of any Entropian stamps that are not represented in this publication, I most sincerely urge you to immediately contact me or the Interplanetary Philatelist Society in Kukursk.

PLANET ENTROPIA

Entropia is a small planet that shares a common sun with 11 other moons in a constellation named the Great Cosmic Disorder. Entropia contains only one major continent and five bigger islands. The continent is partially divided by the Bay of Takashiro and surrounded by the Gulf of the Deep and the Northern Sea.

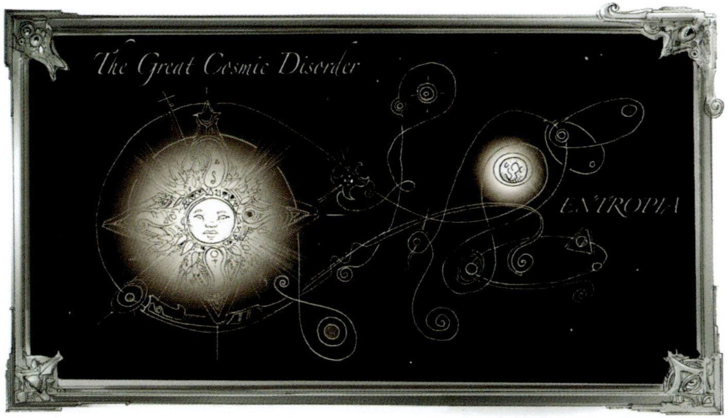

ENTROPIA'S POPULATION AND HISTORY

Millions of years ago, thousands of species emerged from the preprotozoan forest. In comparison with animal species on other planets, many of the creatures were, to different degrees, sentient, meaning they had the ability to speak and create. Two dominant species emerged—the humanoid Entropians and the aquatic Axolotls. Over time, Entropians became the dominant species on dry land while Axolotls controlled the oceans. The dream monk Taka the Fifth introduced Entropia to its current lunar year calendar and the first dated seals. Stamps have only existed on Entropia for the last 300 lunar years. During this time, Entropia transitioned from a feudal political system to a direct democracy. This time period is also marked by the great Oceanic Wars. Most of the stamps in the following collection were produced during the lifetime of Queen Pingo the Young and document Entropian life, culture, and major historical events.

LUNAR YEAR	EVENT
899	Orlando the Insane discovers gunpowder
911	Birkenwurst-Cornichon Peace Bridge
945	First private school for the Occult and Bizzare opens
951	The Bathing Giants are discovered
959	Great Typhoon strikes during Marquis de Salade's 29th birthday celebration
963	Moon Shadow 1 nearly plunges into the icy waters; Results in transport of pets only being allowed in specially-designed travel bags
977	Princess Pingo is born
981	Solar Eclipse; Nunzio discovers the secret of the gondola airships Winter Games held at Ice Royale
984	Princess Pingo's parents die in the disaster of Balloon City Three; She gains the official title Queen Pingo the Young
993	First solo trans-oceanic flight by Queen Pingo
999	Equinox declared Rain Forest Capital of Entropia
1001	Underground Kitchen Fire Reign of the Childish Robot Czar begins (10 years long)
1005	Minicows of Kukursk appear
1011	Childish Robot Czar and Animatronic Shock Troops' occupation of Entropia ends; Entropia becomes a democracy. First Recreational Nature Preserve, Lake Rabbit Tooth, created by Queen Pingo Moon Cowboys and Cowgirls gain freedom
1012	Queen Pingo declares Backpack Penguins illegal
1013	Lightning Ziggurats of Tukar discovered
1016	Queen Pingo the Young becomes first Entropian to visit the Whale Cities of the Deep

OPPOSITE: ENTROPIA'S GEOGRAPHY UNDER THE RULE OF QUEEN PINGO THE YOUNG

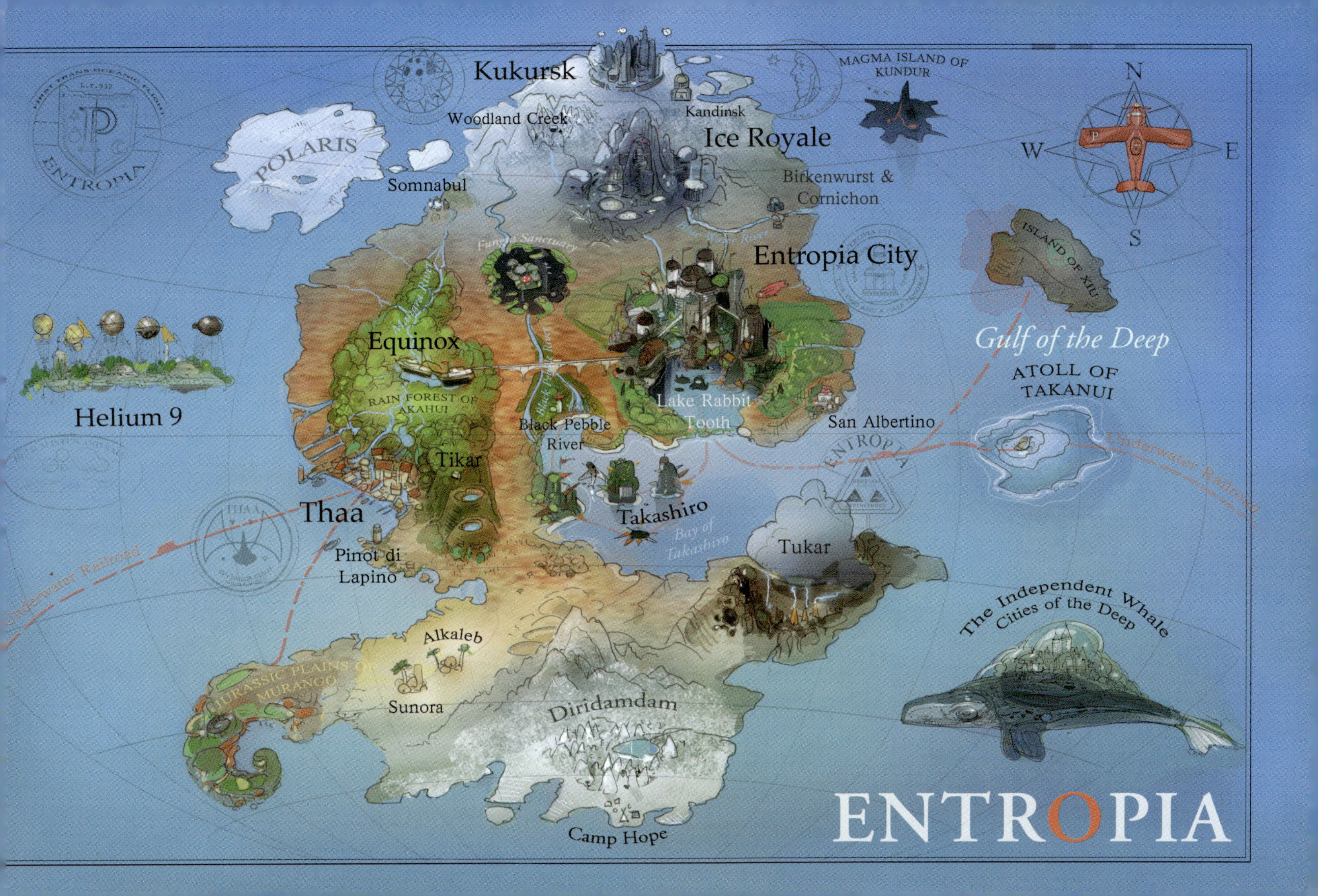

FIRST TRANS-OCEANIC FLIGHT
L.Y. 932
ENTROPIA
Kukursk
Woodland Creek
Kandinsk
MAGMA ISLAND OF KUNDUR
Ice Royale
N
W
E
S
POLARIS
Somnabul
Birkenwurst & Cornichon
Fungus Sanctuary
Blue Water River
Entropia City
ISLAND OF XIU
Equinox
Gulf of the Deep
ATOLL OF TAKANUI
RAIN FOREST OF AKAHUI
Helium 9
Lake Rabbit Tooth
Black Pebble River
San Albertino
ENTROPIA
Underwater Railroad
Tikar
Thaa
THAA
Takashiro
Bay of Takashiro
Tukar
Pinot di Lapino
Underwater Railroad
The Independent Whale Cities of the Deep
Alkaleb
JURASSIC PLAINS OF MURANGO
Sunora
Diridamdam
Camp Hope
ENTROPIA

The Bay of Takashiro is famous for its magnificent breaching Firefish. During spring nights, they can be seen jumping up to 150 feet in the air, trailing a tail of glowing bioluminescent plasma behind them.

It is the glowing plasma—not the Firefish—that the fisherwomen skillfully harvest with their plasma skimmers. Their dangerous challenge is to get as close as possible to a breaching Firefish immediately after it jumps and skim the precious bioluminescent plasma from the ocean's surface.

Glowing plasma is Takashiro's most precious commodity and is sold in lamps all over Entropia.

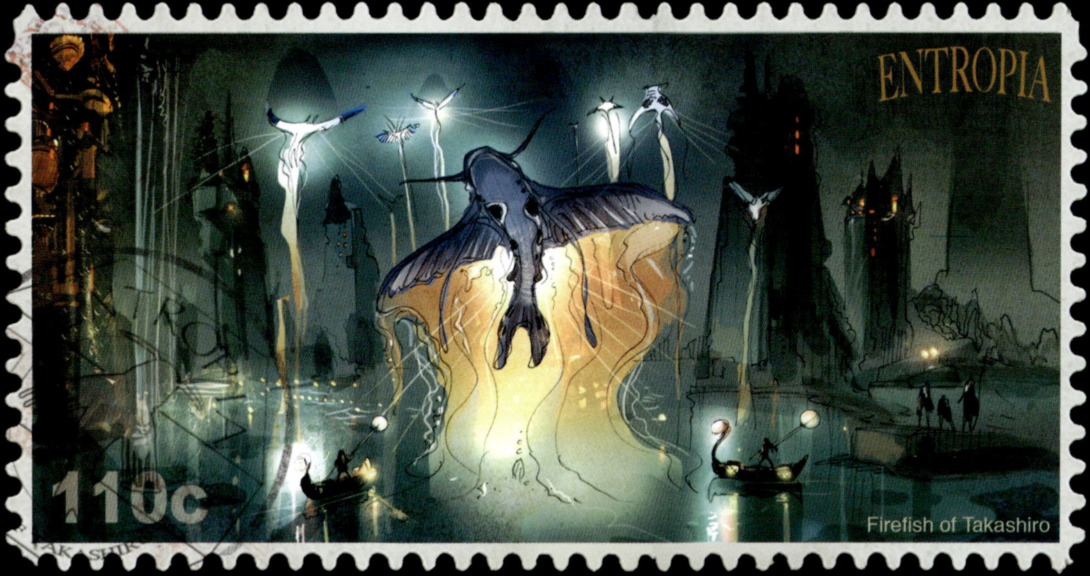

110c *The Firefish of Takashiro*

PROMOTIONAL STAMP

On the second full moon after the winter solstice, Entropia celebrates the new year with elaborate festivals throughout the country. In major cities such as Entropia City and Ice Royale, spectacular fireworks are launched from airships and boats, and thousands of nakacrackers are lit to cast out evil spirits. In the southern provinces of Takashiro and Thaa, the festivities often take on a more thoughtful tone, with elaborate lantern festivals and mystical night walks commemorating the spirits of the deceased.

Some of the most original rites, however, have been witnessed in the alpine valleys of Kukursk, where village women disguised as tree spirits perform a mystical dance to chase out the winter demons. The demons are traditionally represented by young children, who wear pine costumes, wield giant icicles, and wear particularly ugly masks.

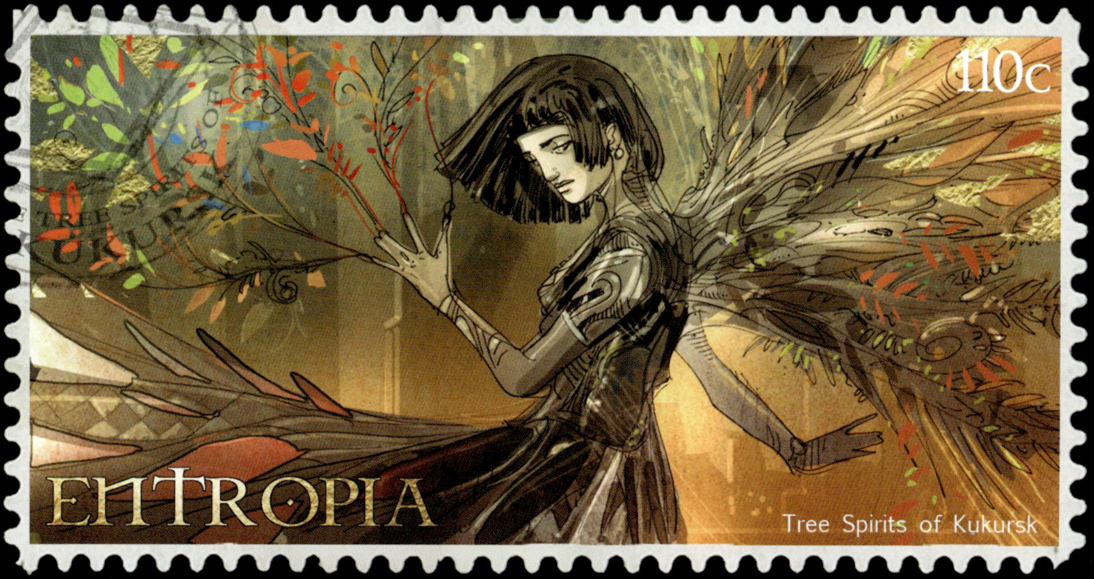

110c *Tree Spirits of Kukursk*
CEREMONIAL STAMP

During one of her night flights over central Entropia, Queen Pingo was forced to make an emergency landing in a potato-corn plantation where she met a strange group of farmers that were half-Entropian and half-animal. The family of Anwar, a young Moon Cowboy, took care of her broken arm and warmly hosted her. During this fateful encounter, the Queen became strongly aware of the social inequalities plaguing her country, and from that day made promoting peace and friendship between the sentient animals and the Entropians her priority.

As a token of her sincerity, she refused to wear the Entropian crown and instead was often seen with bright-red prosthetic horns and her signature animal tattoos. She supported the Moon Cowboys and Cowgirls in their fight for freedom, which they eventually gained in lunar year 1011.

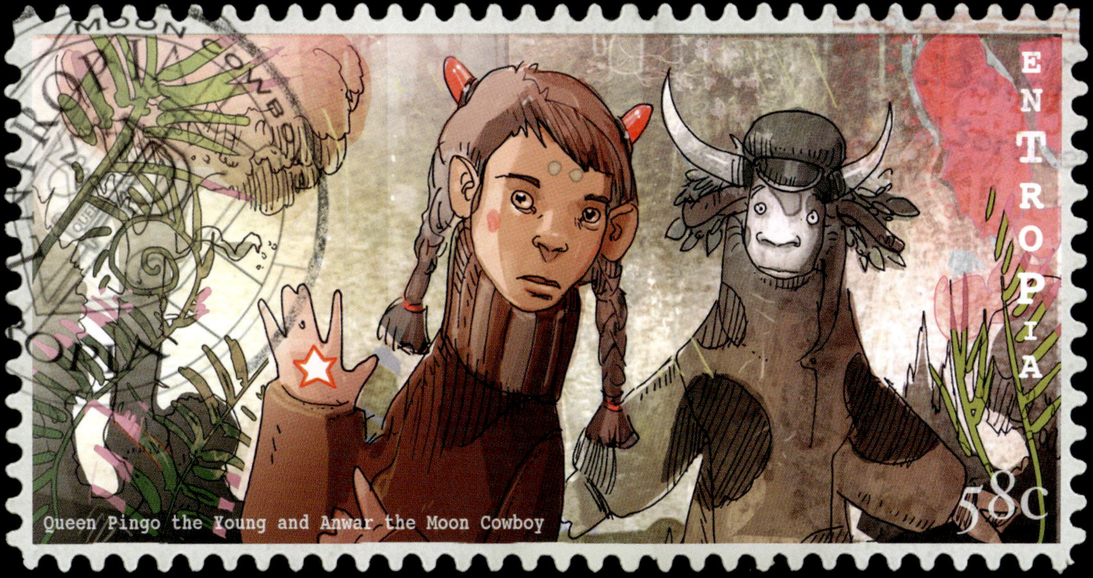

58c *Queen Pingo the Young and Anwar the Moon Cowboy*

FRIENDSHIP STAMP

It is widely known that Entropia City croissants are the world's tastiest, but only a few people know who is responsible for such delight. They call themselves the Secret Guild of Croissant Bakers. In Entropia City's underground kitchens, near the perpetually burning volcano ovens, the bakers and their magical fire lemurs dedicate their entire lives to the creation of pastries and other secret things.

It has been speculated that the guild had its hand in the creation of the Childish Robot Czar and his Animatronics, but an investigation was dropped as all evidence was destroyed in the Great Underground Kitchen Fire of lunar year 1001.

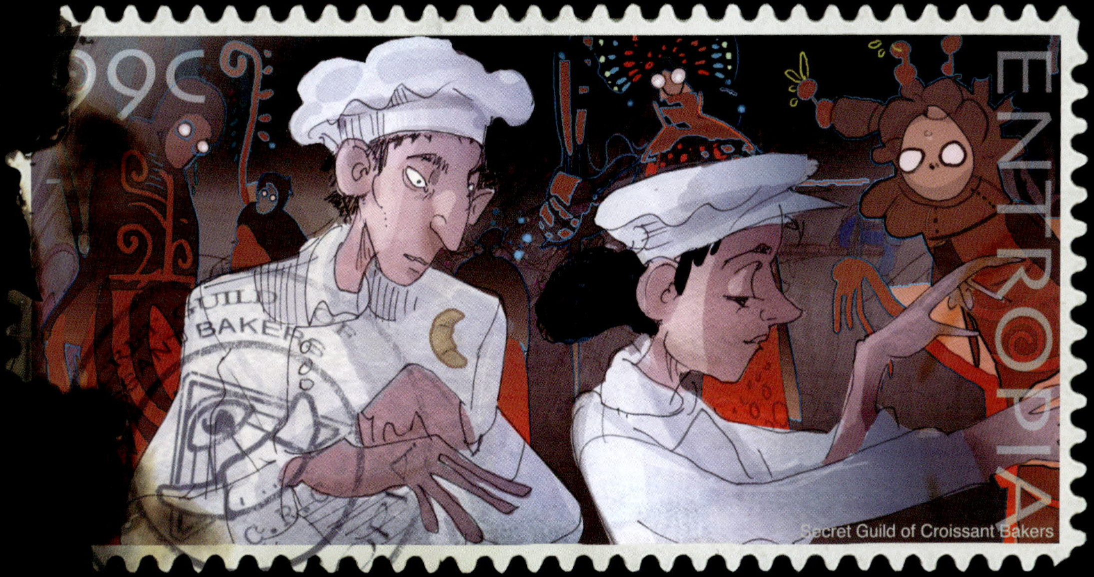

99c *The Secret Guild of Croissant Bakers*

COMMEMORATIVE STAMP

In lunar year 1027, Françoise de Chantilly founded Entropia's first modern dance ensemble to protest the rigid ballets that were popular at the time. The formerly lavish sets were replaced with what Françoise called Stage-ersatz, which consisted of a black empty stage decorated with only two chairs. Tutus and ballet shoes were shed and replaced with black leotards and turtlenecks.

In her first mise-en-scène, entitled ***Immobile***, Françoise challenged the preconceived artistic notions of visibly perplexed spectators when her dance troupe stood still on stage, holding the same pose, for an agonizing 90 minutes. For five more years, she shocked audiences with her "black phase," until a trip to the countryside inspired her to create yet another new form of dance. This one was influenced by the traditional tribal dances of Entropia. Her self-proclaimed ballet masterpiece, ***I'm a Turkey, You're a Tree***, became her first critically acclaimed success.

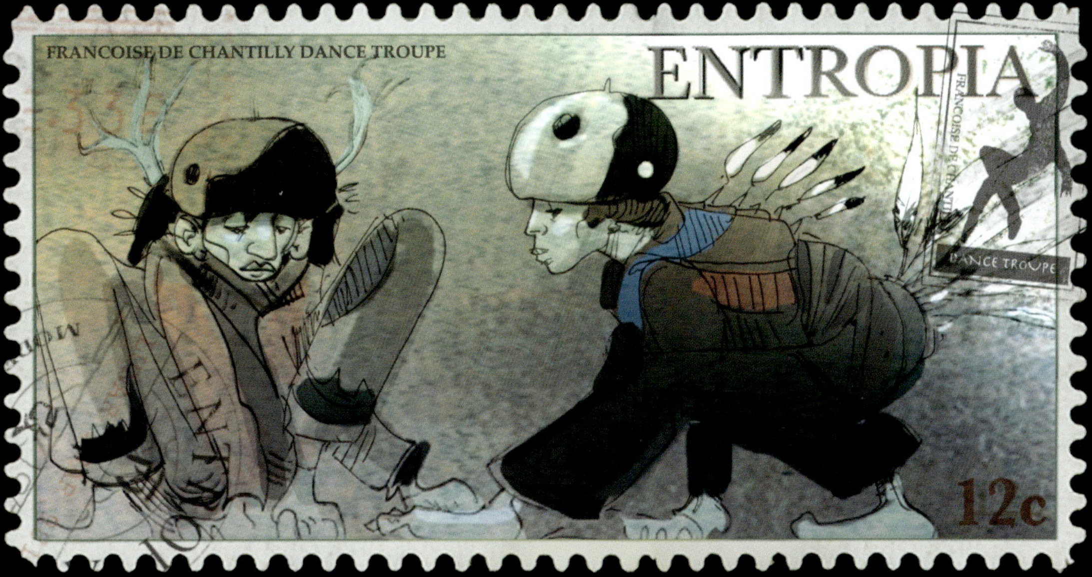

12c *Françoise de Chantilly Dance Troupe*

COMMEMORATIVE STAMP

Years of attempts to make cities fly using balloons filled with Murango gas had proved fruitless. After some of the most devastating accidents in history—namely the disaster of Balloon City Three, which exploded in an infernal ball of fire—Nunzio Helium, a young scientist from the Royal Institute for Science Without Magic, discovered a noncombustible gas, making balloon cities safe for future generations.

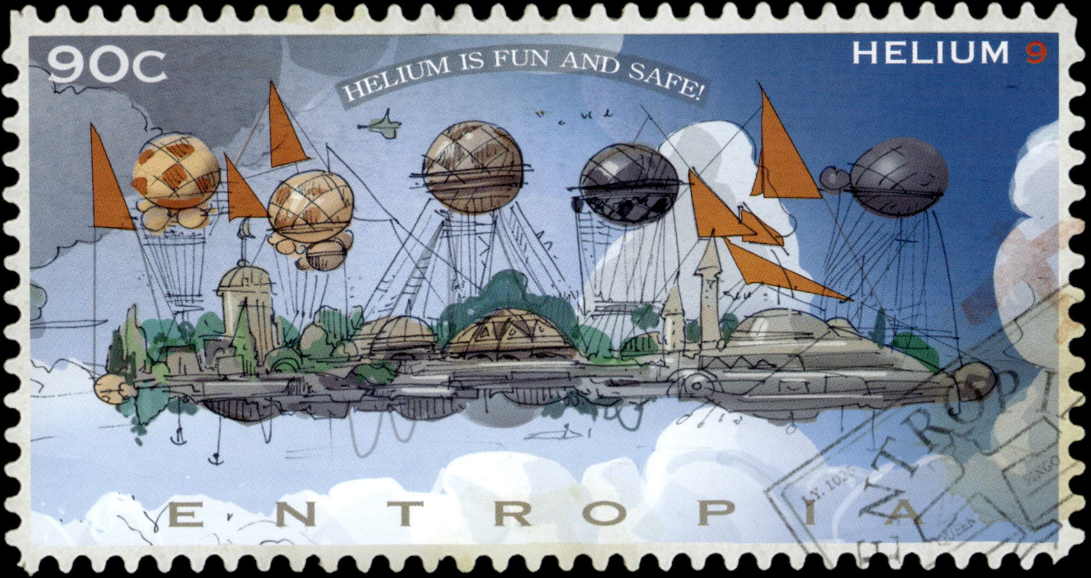

90c *Helium Nine*

JUBILATION STAMP

Entropia's oceans are famous for their astonishing biodiversity. In addition to many traditional ocean inhabitants, Entropia's sea life also consists of the "mirror species." Entropian zoologists made the intriguing discovery that for every species on land, there exists an aquatic counterpart (for example, sea horses, sea bears, sea birds, sea hares, and so on). Every four years, the most sportive ocean creatures meet for the Great Underwater Derby, circling once around the enormous atoll of Takanui. The race is generally dominated by traditional aquatic favorites such as dolphins and speed barracudas. In the spring of lunar year 935, however, an ocean outsider, the field rabbit Geronimo Flash, won the derby for the first time. Since he had to surface for air more frequently than his aquatic competitors, Flash was at a clear disadvantage, but he won the race thanks to his unwavering spirit and a special technique that involved a secret, propeller-like movement using his rabbit ears.

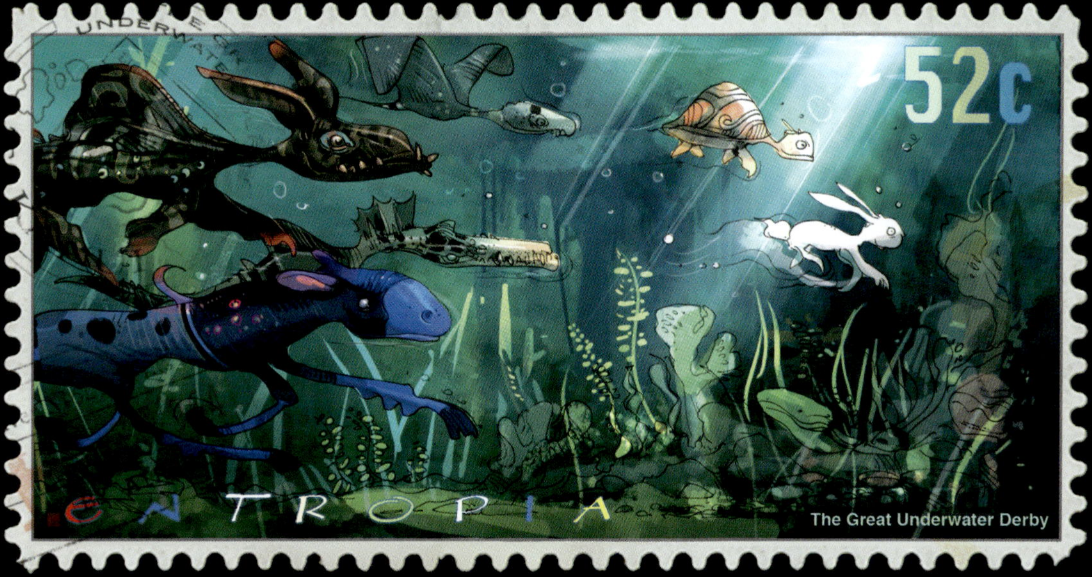

52c *The Great Underwater Derby*

ATHLETIC ACHIEVEMENT STAMP

Due to Entropia's love affair with the butter croissant and the consumption of extremely rich food, many Entropians in the capitals suffer from high blood pressure and are developing heart failure early in life. For that reason, in lunar year 996 Queen Pingo the Young spearheaded a medical campaign to raise awareness of the importance of a healthy heart under the slogan, "Take care of your heart, you only have one."

The slogan took on a life of its own when it served as inspiration for the lyrics of the smash-hit opera ***Lovely, Take Care of Your Heart***, which was first performed by the Two-and-a-Half Tenors in the Royal Opera House of Entropia City.

It must be noted that these lyrics were changed by a group of insolent children who rhymed: "Take care of your heart, you only have one, except for Axolotls who have two and Animatronics who have none."

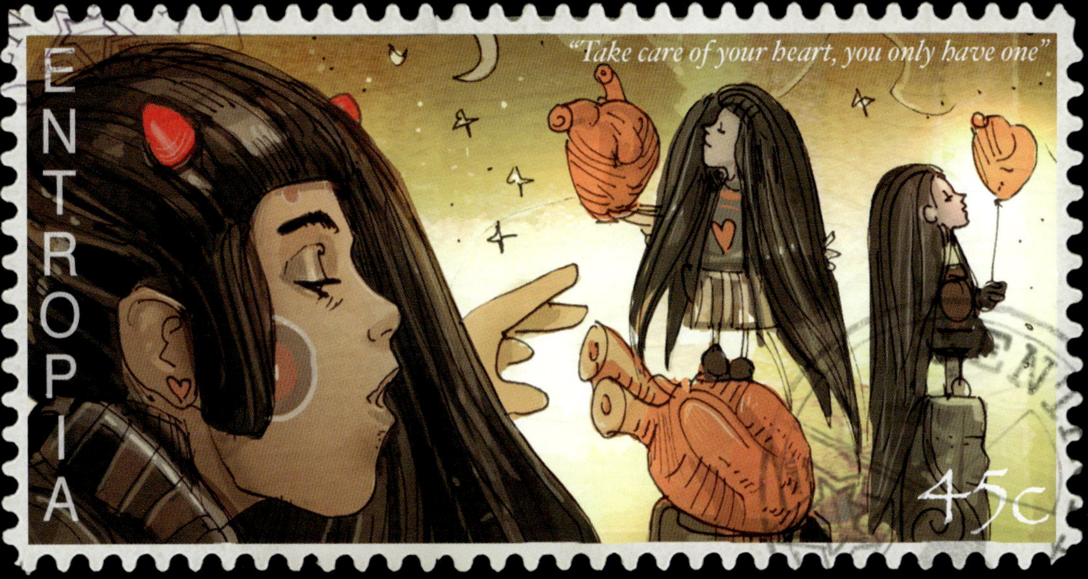

45c *Take Care of Your Heart*

HEALTH-AWARENESS STAMP

For many Entropians, the word "vacation" is synonymous with the colorful Twin Cities of Equinox.

The Twin Cities were founded after the cruise ships Equinox I and II became hopelessly stuck in the Manara River in the heart of the tropical rain forest of Akahui. After several failed rescue attempts, the Entropian government decided to connect the stranded ships with the construction of a daring air-rail. Equinox has become so popular that in lunar year 999 the region was declared Rain Forest Capital of Entropia.

It should be noted, however, that no tourist ever leaves the elevated safety of the Twin Cities for fear of the roaming Wilderbeasts and a mysterious tribe of dragonfly hunters.

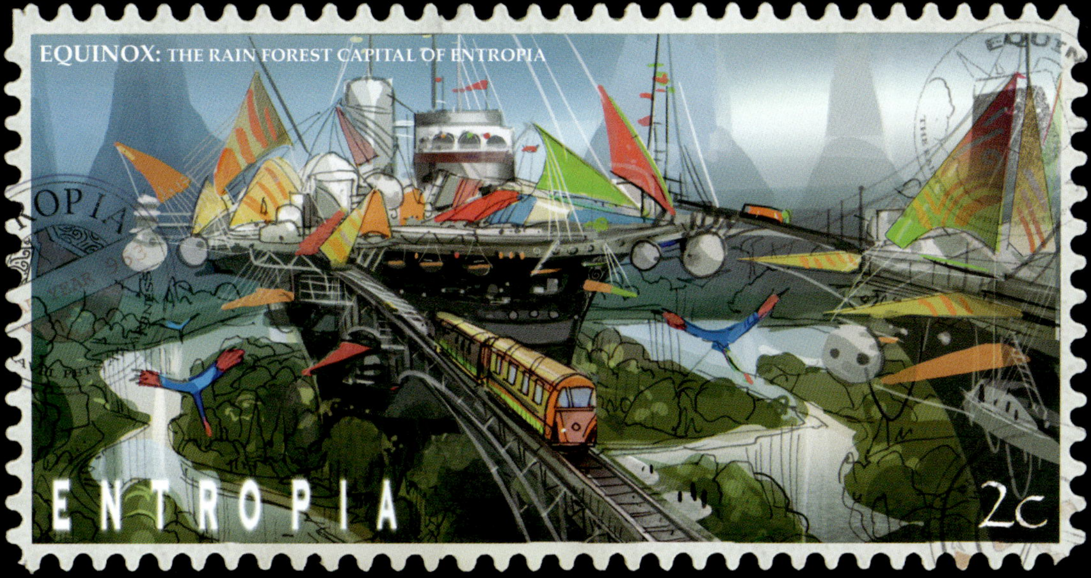

2c *Equinox: Rain Forest Capital of Entropia*

PROMOTIONAL STAMP

The two brothers Mauro and Ototo and their half-sister Esmeralda grew up in a deprived household in the outskirts of Entropia City. Their parents were part of the Secret Guild of Croissant Bakers and were hardly ever at home. To occupy themselves during this time of parental neglect, the three siblings began singing popular operas in their backyard. Their lives changed for the better when their evil parents were killed in a mysterious kitchen fire, and after numerous auditions, they got the leading roles for the opera ***Lovely, Take Care of Your Heart.***

Due to the phenomenal success of their debut opera, the siblings achieved universal acclaim and for a decade toured Entropia's opera houses as the Two-and-a-Half Tenors. In later years, Ototo died of heart failure, most likely due to his croissant addiction. Mauro stopped singing altogether and married a beautiful fisherwoman in Takashiro, and Esmeralda, who always resented being the "half-tenor," tried unsuccessfully to launch a solo career under the name Esmeralda, the Nightingale of Entropia.

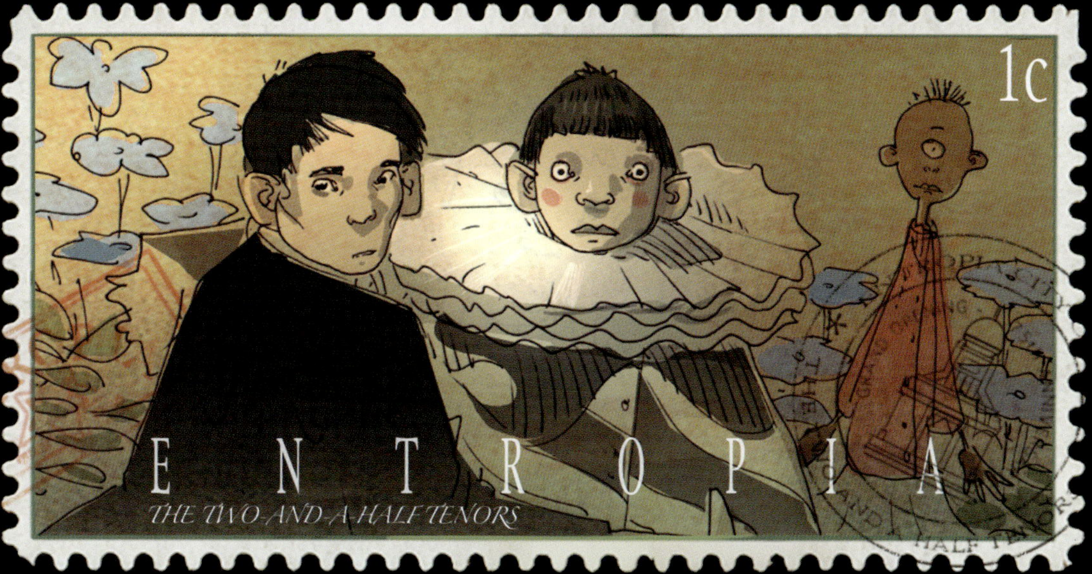

1c *The Two-and-a-Half Tenors*

MUSIC-APPRECIATION STAMP

High above the picturesque fishing villages of the Entropian Riviera stands the rose monastery of San Albertino. Its sun-exposed location and the volcanic soil underneath it are perfect for growing Entropia's world-class roses. For centuries, San Albertino's rose monks have been perfecting their craft, and orders pile up daily from clients all over Entropia. In order to move the very fragile roses from the monastery to remote clients, the monks use domestic carrier spiders to transport the living roses in their moist, earthy headpieces. The spiders run at speeds of up to 60 miles per hour and, for an additional fee, will perform an event-appropriate delivery dance upon arrival.

Despite the fact that the roses can be rush-ordered day or night, a trip to the Rose Monastery and its surroundings is a wonderful idea. The fish dishes in the nearby villages are simple and delicious, and the desserts, such as rose-honey ice cream, are very tasty.

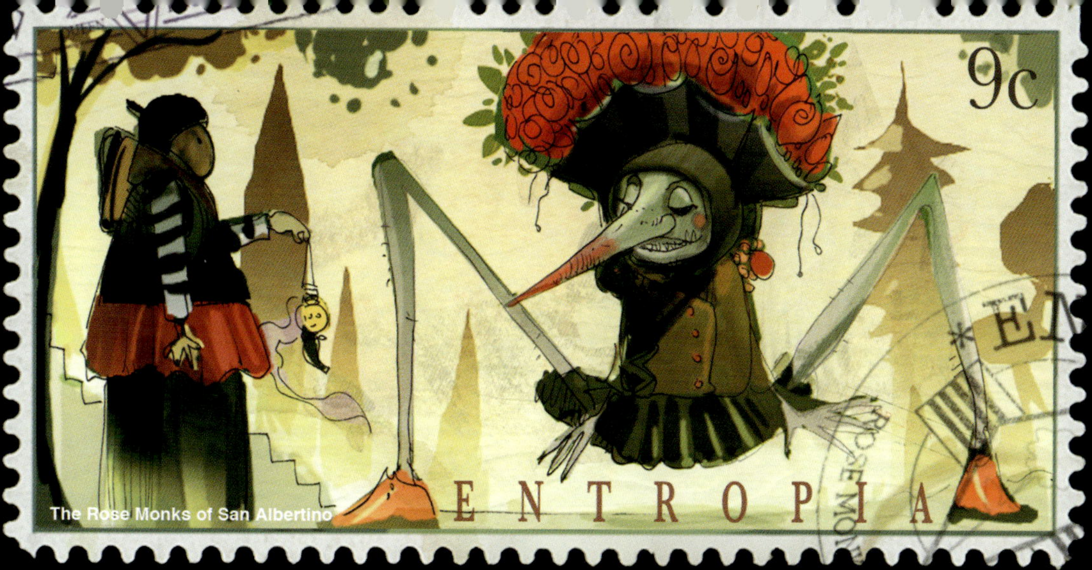

9c *The Rose Monks of San Albertino*

PROMOTIONAL STAMP

Princess Pingo was very little when her parents died in the infernal accident of Balloon City Three, leaving her with the official title Queen Pingo the Young.

She was raised by her loving Aunt Pongo and her equally adoring yet eccentric Uncle Eugenio. Aunt Pongo's mission was to raise a sensible, well-rounded young queen with a good heart and a smart brain, so Uncle Eugenio did his best to counter his sister's traditional education with his own philosophies of artistic exuberance and the power of imagination. As an example of their differences, Uncle Eugenio once offered his old biplane to the princess on her eleventh birthday. Aunt Pongo was not pleased, but after endless debate, Queen Pingo was finally allowed to keep the plane under the condition that she take proper flying lessons.

After the local air academies rejected the Queen for being too young, in addition to her being a small girl, Aunt Pongo tracked down a very gifted flight instructor, young Nunzio Helium, for private lessons. Not only did he turn Queen Pingo into an excellent pilot, he also modified her old plane using his own designs. At age 13, the young queen broke the Entropian speed record and on her sixteenth birthday, she was the first pilot to succeed in flying solo nonstop from Entropia City to Thaa, crossing the Gulf of the Deep.

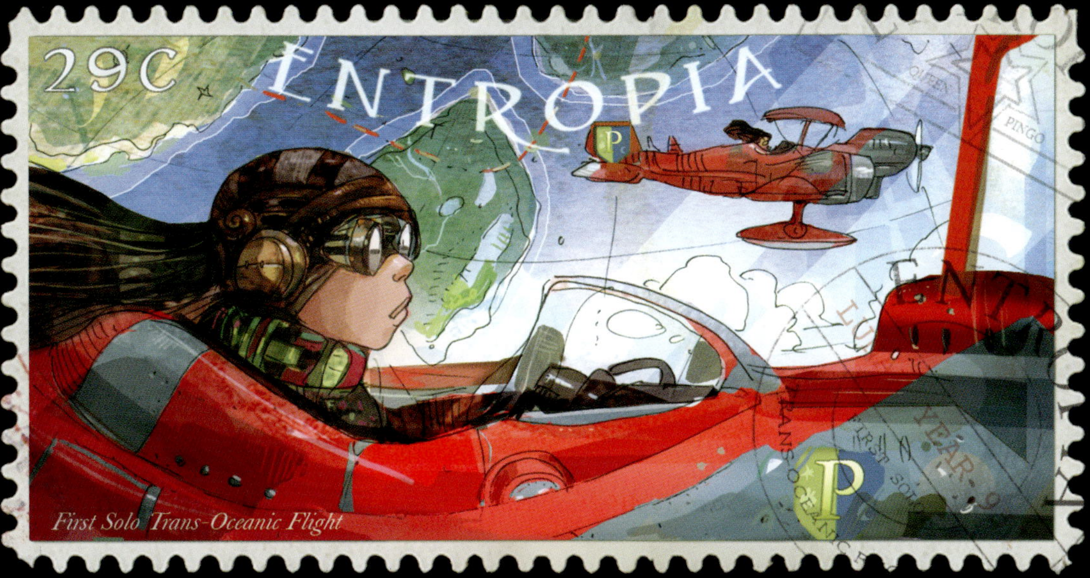

29C ***First Solo Trans-Oceanic Flight***

COMMEMORATIVE STAMP

Deep in the rain forest of Entropia lives one of the most elusive tribes—the Swift-tongued Dragonfly Hunters of Akahui.

Earlier in Entropia's history, the frightening twang of a slingtongue followed by terrifying screamlaughter often struck fear into the hearts of the first merchants and tourists who cruised the Manara River. Reports of a murderous tribe of headshrinkers made their way into the front pages of the newspapers of Entropia City and even as far as Ice Royale. All these hair-raising stories have proven to be untrue, thanks to the reports of Sir Allen Mackenzie of the Royal Ethnology Society of Entropia.

Here is an excerpt from his expedition diary:

"Day 29
After traveling by canoe down the Manara River and walking for two weeks deep into the endless rain forest, I finally made contact with the Akahuis. I initially kept a safe distance to observe them until a group of young hunters made the first contact by greeting me with their traditional screamlaughter. They invited me to join their clan and share a delicious meal of roasted dragonflies. Akahuis have turned out to be one of the most loving and hospitable peoples I have ever met. They have a disarming sense of humor and their up to four-foot-long tongues make them the most phenomenal insect hunters in the world."

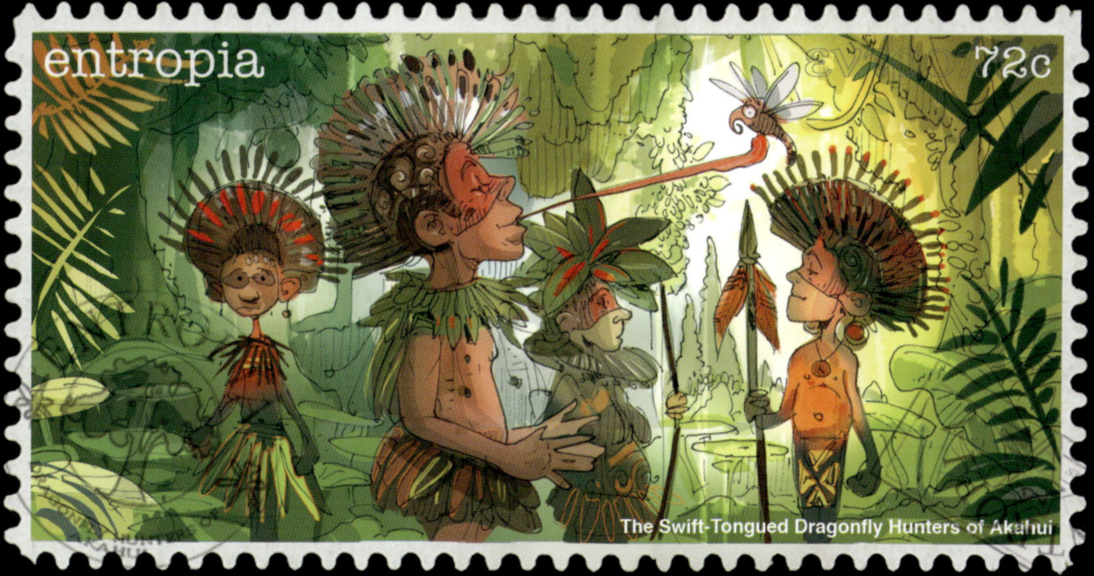

72c *The Swift-Tongued Dragonfly Hunters of Akahui*

EXPLORATION STAMP

Where the Manara River joins the Gulf of the Deep lays the harbor city of Thaa.

Known for its lighthouses, a historic submarine harbor, and a spicy tea made of naka nuts, Thaa also has a unique transportation system that consists of hundreds of levitating gondolas piloted by sky sailors. These floating gondolas have made the city famous all over Entropia.

Every resident stoically maintains that the ships take to the air because of the supernatural chanting of their pilots, who are trained from a very young age in Thaa's levitation schools. The mystery of the levitating ships was exposed during the solar eclipse of lunar year 981, when a curious orphan named Nunzio the Boy Genius broke into one of the airship hangars and discovered that the inner hulls of the gondolas were filled with an unknown gas. He was soon apprehended by a group of infuriated sky sailors and had to make a daring escape involving a bag of naka nuts, a unicycle, and his wooden minisubmarine. Forever banned from his hometown, young Nunzio made his way to Entropia City, where he matriculated into the Royal Institute for Science Without Magic.

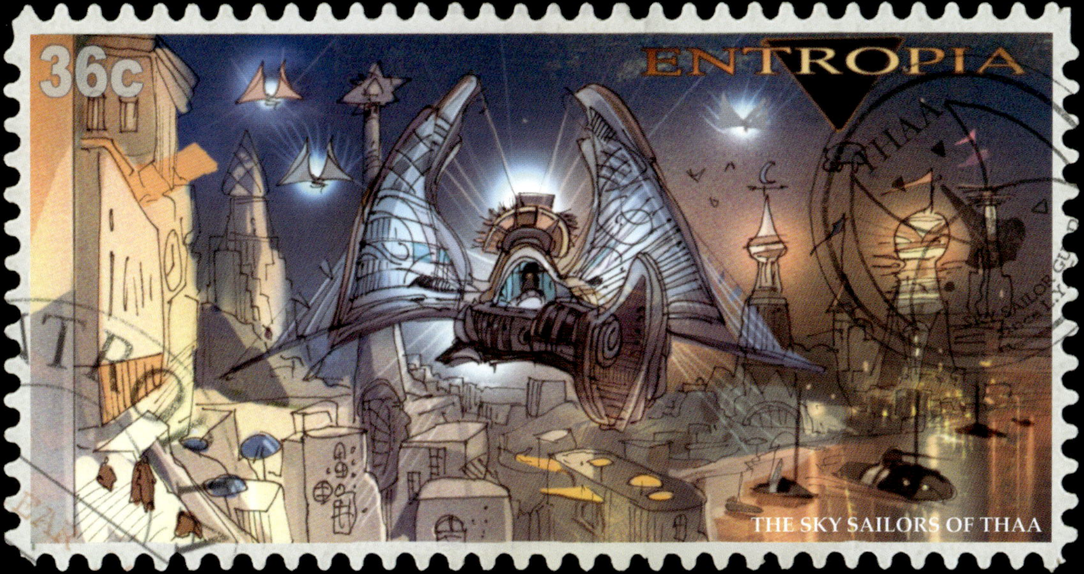

36c *The Sky Sailors of Thaa*

COMMEMORATIVE STAMP

High above the city of Thaa, on fertile volcanic highlands, live the Naka-Nut Farmers of Tikar. For countless generations, naka-nut farming has provided them with a sustainable income. The white naka-nuts are planted during the full moon nights of the first month of the year and grow in bushels underground. Once the autumn harvest is brought in, the farmers descend to the marketplaces of the great city of Thaa to sell their famous goods. Naka is one of the most important Entropian food groups and its applications are endless. It can be consumed raw, roasted, baked, turned into naka butter, boiled in naka soup, or brewed into a delicious and invigorating tea.

There is also a forbidden species of the naka nut that grows deeply hidden in the tropical rain forest bordering the highlands. The crimson nut (*naka hallucinatus*) can only be found with the help of a naka swine, and its sale is punishable by law. The Red Gold, as it is known, is highly addictive and leads its consumers into a sleepless slumber from which many never awaken.

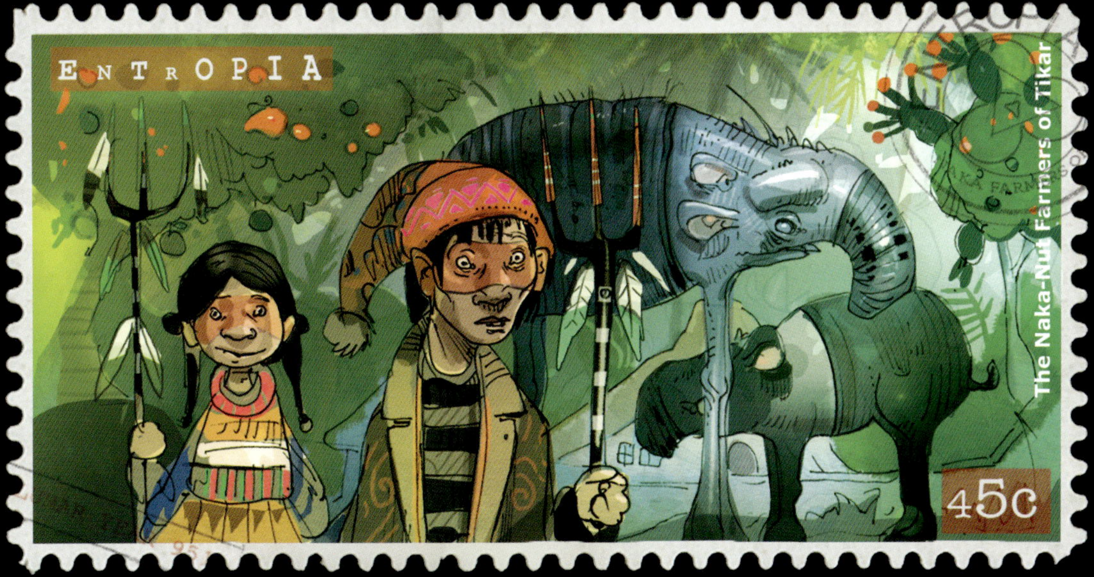

45c *The Naka-Nut Farmers of Tikar*

AGRICULTURAL STAMP

No other animal is dearer to the hearts of Entropians big and small than the Blue-striped Artwark (*porco rothko vermiculus nocturnum*). In previous times, this nocturnal insect eater was almost hunted to extinction by ruthless robot poachers seeking its blue-striped fur pelt.

Today the artwark is under the protection of the Entropian Wildlife Society and has been named National Animal of Entropia by Queen Pingo the Young.

Artwarks make formidable pets. It has been documented that they have the ability to produce art and learn basic speech.

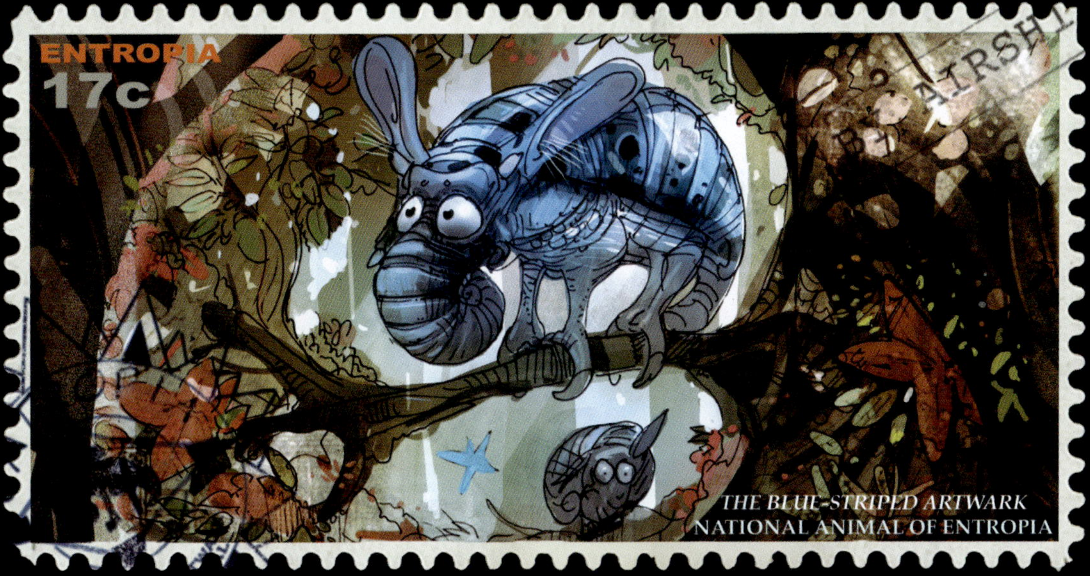

17C *The Blue-Striped Artwark*

APPRECIATION STAMP

The renowned poet Naomi Appletart claims to have spent most of her childhood in a secret underground fern grotto in Takashiro's hinterland. In her memoirs, ***Testimony of an Overtalented Child***, she describes in astonishing detail how she was raised by five ectoplasmic grandmothers, who taught her the language of angels. Nobody knows if her outlandish claims are true, but it doesn't really matter—Entropians can't get enough of her surreal haikus, which are published weekly in the culture section of the ***Entropian Advertiser.***

"Haiku"
By Naomi Appletart

Drip 8, Drip 5, Drip 27
In the moist grotto I used to play lotto,
With my five grandmothers and my cat Toto.
Nobody won.

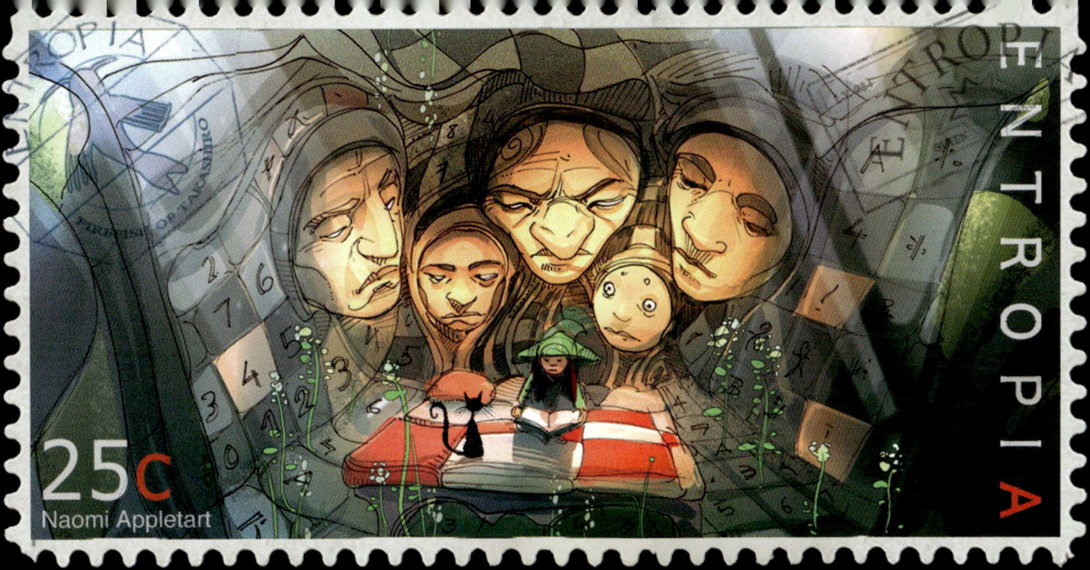

25c *Naomi Appletart*

POET LAUREATE STAMP

For his twenty-ninth birthday, Marquis de Salade, whose life motto has always been "Too much is never enough," ordered his majordomo, Nepumuk, the third chief steward of his larger household, to create a celebration the likes of which the world had never seen before.

The plan was for a floating parade of 29 specially fabricated birthday galleons to make a seven-hour journey down the Black Pebble River. Fifteen different banquets featuring delicacies from each province of Entropia were to be loaded on floating rafts. No expense was to be spared. The highlight of the evening, and of Nepumuk's long-standing career, was the creation of a unique river symphony. Two thousand handcrafted porcelain heads were special-ordered from the best craftsmen of underwater music, located in distant Takashiro. Each head, once placed in the riverbed, was able to produce one distinct melodic sound. For over four months, the heads were carefully positioned and tuned so that a boat traveling four knots would experience a magnificent symphony created uniquely by the power of water—***Nepumuk's River Symphony Deluxe***.

However, one day before the celebration, disaster struck and all of central Entropia was hit by the great typhoon of lunar year 959. Fortunately, nobody was hurt when the entire fleet of galleons and the 15 food rafts sunk to the bottom of the riverbed—nobody, that is, except Nepumuk, who disappeared during the storm and was never found. People from Black Pebble River claim the majordomo has joined the aquatic chorus as the eternal conductor of his 2,000 singing heads.

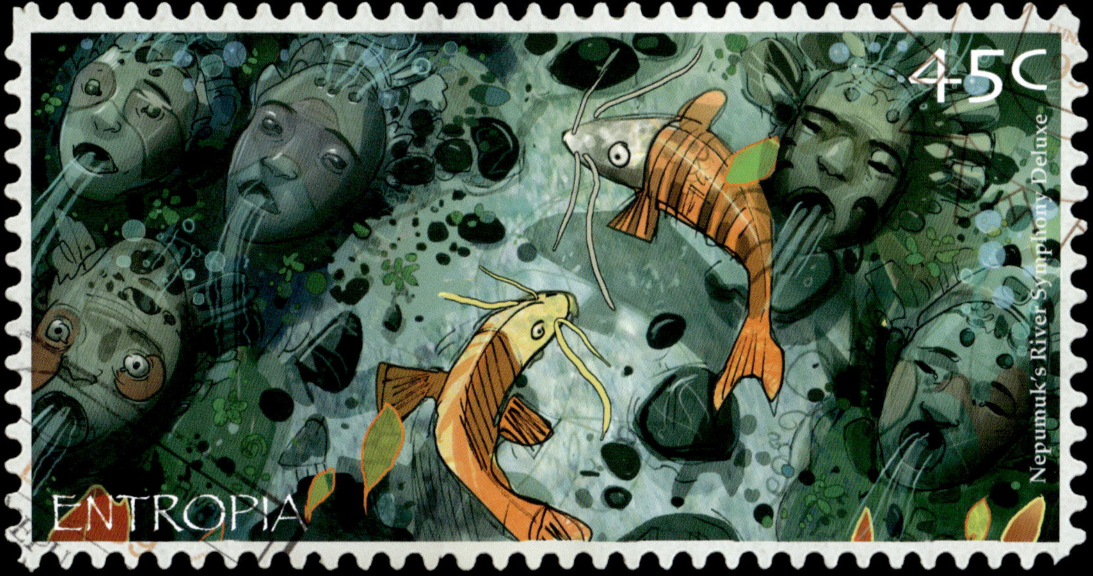

45c ***Nepumuk's River Symphony Deluxe***

COMMEMORATIVE STAMP

If winter sport with unwavering class is your idea of a vacation, a trip to the northern city of Ice Royale is an absolute must.

Winter tourists from all over Entropia flock to Ice Royale to enjoy the year-round skiing, skating, and first-class dining. The starting point of 90 miles of phenomenal ski slopes is located on the top floor of the Metropolitan Hotel. Guests who stay in one of the luxury suites can access the slopes directly from their own private balconies, ski into the city center, enjoy a Takashiro caviar cocktail, hit the powder once again, and end their day 10,000 feet below in one of the seven star restaurants on the romantic shores of Ice Royale's frozen lakes. Returning to the suites is easy thanks to the world's fastest elevator, which was constructed exclusively for the Winter Games of lunar year 981.

While visiting the city, it is advised to avoid conversing about the Winter Games to any of the locals. The beloved local ski team's crushing defeat by a team of rabbits, who came from a tiny logging village on Entropia's outer rim, left their pride injured for many years to follow.

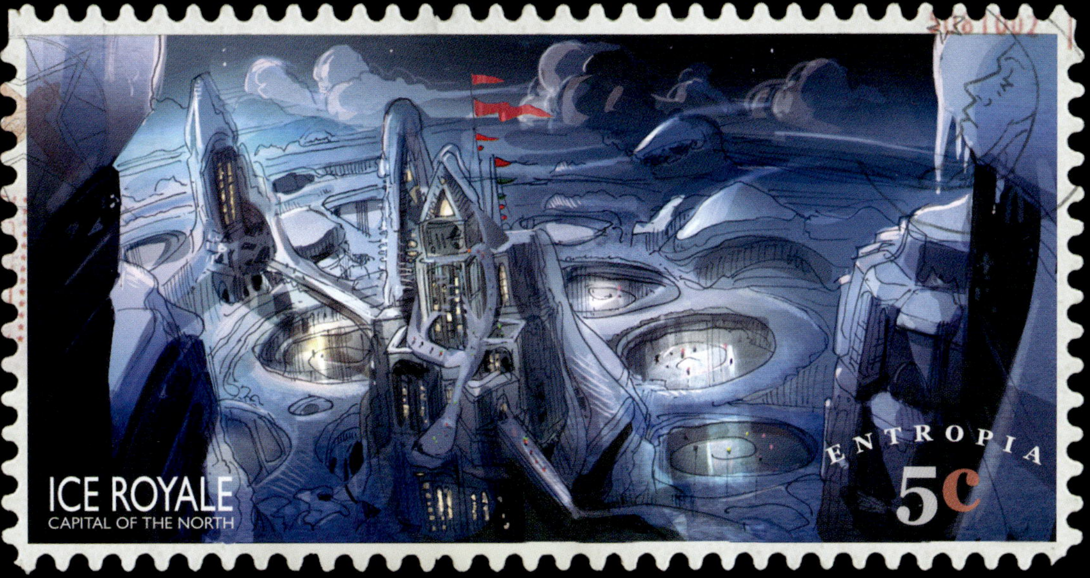

5c *Ice Royale: Capital of the North*
PROMOTIONAL STAMP

In Entropia, no celebration is complete without a fireworks display of some sort.

Centuries ago, the first firecrackers were created by roasting green naka nuts in their shells, which would explode with a loud bang. The nakacrackers were soon used in funerals and weddings to scare away evil spirits and ghosts. In lunar year 899, the infamous alchemist Orlando the Insane discovered gunpowder and sold his discovery to the highest bidder. His life briskly ended when he blew himself up while attempting to build exploding locks. The only good that came from his inventions was that black powder allowed for the creation of more and more sophisticated fireworks.

The most beautiful pyrotechnic creations can be seen in the annual fireworks fair of Kukursk, where pyrologists and fire wizards show off their latest creations. Visitors of the fair have to sign a strict affidavit stating that the festival's organizers are not liable for the participants getting burned, blown up, or mutilated in any way. Surprisingly, the fairs have been mostly accident-free, except for a group of firemonks who, while performing mind-defying acrobatics, instantaneously combusted.

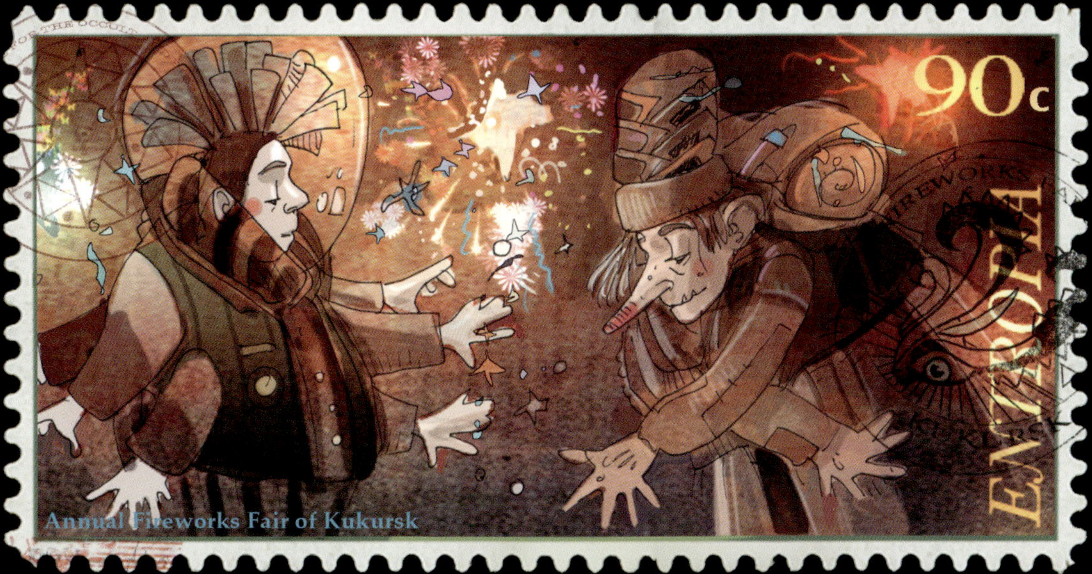

90c *The Annual Fireworks Fair of Kukursk*

PROMOTIONAL STAMP

Gwendolyn and the Lobsterman are two prominent characters appearing in Entropia's mythology. The tragic love story is found in hundreds of versions, but the basic storyline is always the same. Princess Gwendolyn is courted by the Lobsterman; he tries to steal her soul but she ends up stealing his heart. In Entropian folklore, death is symbolized by the Lobsterman, who, with his magic lobster scissors, cuts the spiritual cord between body and soul. At the end of the story, Gwendolyn uses the power of love to defy death.

Queen Pingo was a very young girl when she first saw a play about the two lovers performed in the Entropian Royal Theater. Accompanying her to the theater were her parents, who were killed shortly after in a tragic accident that occurred during the inauguration of Balloon City Three. The Lobsterman, Queen Pingo writes in her memoirs, has haunted her dreams throughout most of her childhood.

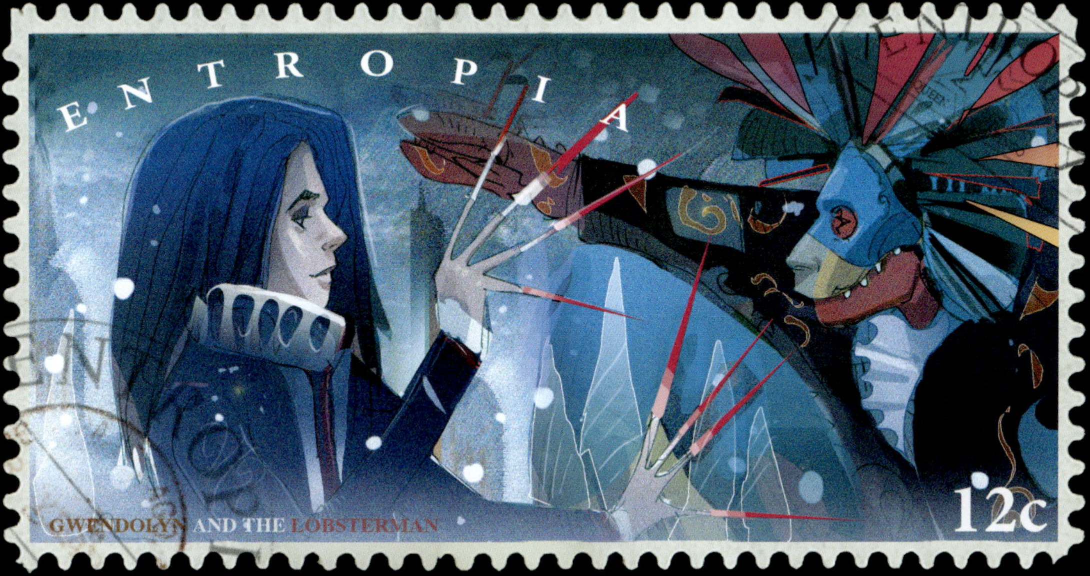

12c *Gwendolyn and the Lobsterman*

MYTHOLOGY STAMP

Along with the naka nut, potato-corn is one of the most important foods of Entropia. Potato-corn is a fantastically versatile plant, which produces high-quality corn above ground and a potatolike turnip underground. Unfortunately, this vegetable is also connected to one of the most shameful chapters in Entropia's history: Entropia's forgotten Moon Farmers.

The so-called Moon Cowboys and Cowgirls were for centuries forced to work on potato-corn plantations with minimal pay and under appalling conditions.

As they could not be classified as Entropian or as animal, they were overlooked by Entropian jurisdiction and Entropia's Wildlife Society. This sad fact was ruthlessly exploited by a group of plantation owners who kept their cheap labor a secret from Entropia's authorities by having them only work at night. Hence the name Moon Farmers.

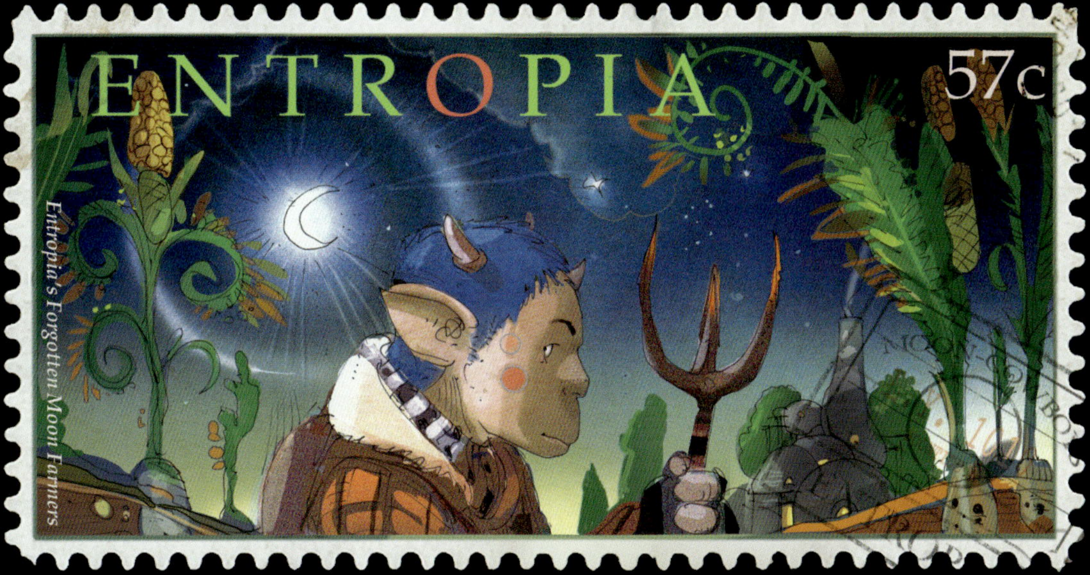

57c *Entropia's Forgotten Moon Farmers*

APPRECIATION STAMP

In lunar year 911, Entropia was hit by the coldest winter of all time. It was so cold that many of the rivers and lakes froze, even those in the warmer provinces. This was also the case for the Bluewater River, which separates the two small rivaling towns of Birkenwurst and Cornichon. These twin towns had ceased having diplomatic relations for more than three decades.

That winter, townspeople from both sides of the frozen river used the opportunity to go ice-skating. As soon as they met, arguments began about the correct way of skating. The townspeople from Birkenwurst used modern skates designed by the local blacksmith, Otto the Wart, while those from Cornichon skated the traditional way, with pairs of eight-day-old baguettes attached to their feet.

The blacksmith started the argument by shouting that the smell of old bread attracted the stink-crows, while Cornichon's mayor retaliated that the only things that stunk on the river were the armpits of the blacksmith's wife…and so the fighting began. After three weeks of brawling, which included two broken legs, one severed finger, and countless knocked-out teeth, the fighting came to a brisk end when the ice broke, pulling the blacksmith's and mayor's sons to the river's bottom. When the townspeople saw the children floating downstream, trapped under the ice, everyone started to work together for the first time in 30 years. The two lucky boys were eventually saved by the blacksmith's heavyset wife, who chopped through the ice with an axe.

That winter, the people of the two towns made amends, and in the spring they built a bridge over the Bluewater River and named it the Birkenwurst-Cornichon Peace Bridge.

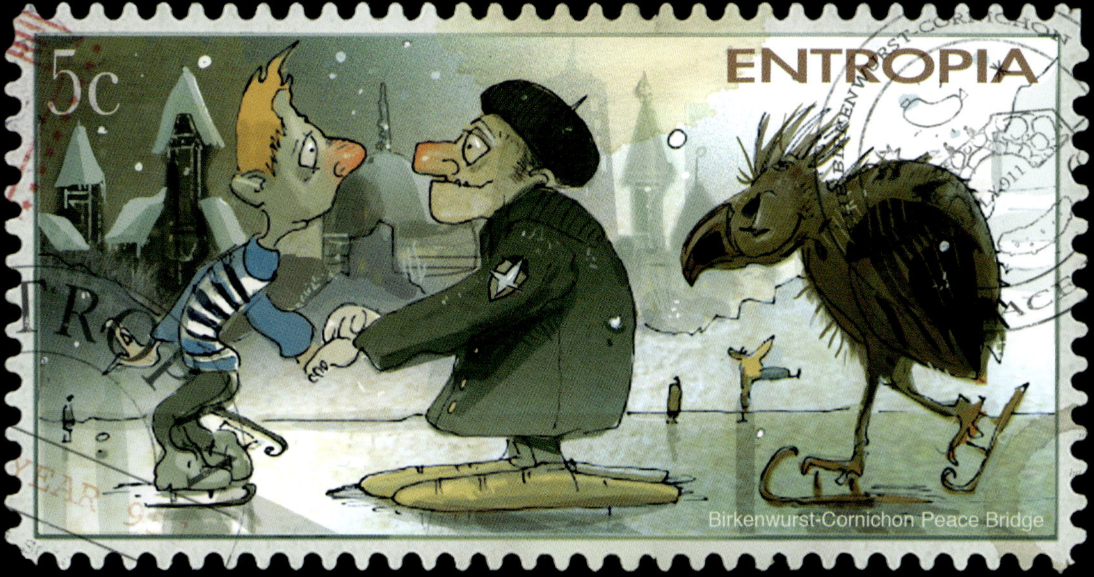

5c *Birkenwurst-Cornichon Peace Bridge*

COMMEMORATIVE STAMP

T*he Moon Lovers* painting propelled Silvia Vega to instant artistic stardom. When the small painting was auctioned off, it sold for the astronomical price of 50,000 Entropian crowns to the notorious Marquis de Salade.

Famous art critic, Sir John Igglesworth, wrote in the ***Entropian Gazette***: "Silvia Vega has moved from the genres of traditional landscape and portrait painting into a completely original and new artistic direction. Escaping her rigid style of yesteryear, she plunges us into a liberating and quasimelodic neosurrealist world, making her one of the top artists to watch."

The scandal broke when Silvia Vega's housekeeper leaked to the press that it was not Vega who painted her surreal masterpieces but her pet artwark, which she kept locked up night and day in a damp and badly heated room. The Entropian Wildlife Society liberated the imprisoned artistic artwark and placed him in the care of a loving foster family who named him Andrew. Vega was banned from all artistic circles and ended up bitter and alone, while Andrew became the first nationally recognized artwark painter. He had a string of highly successful solo shows and with his massive fortune founded O.H.A.N.P., or the Organization to Help Abused and Neglected Pets.

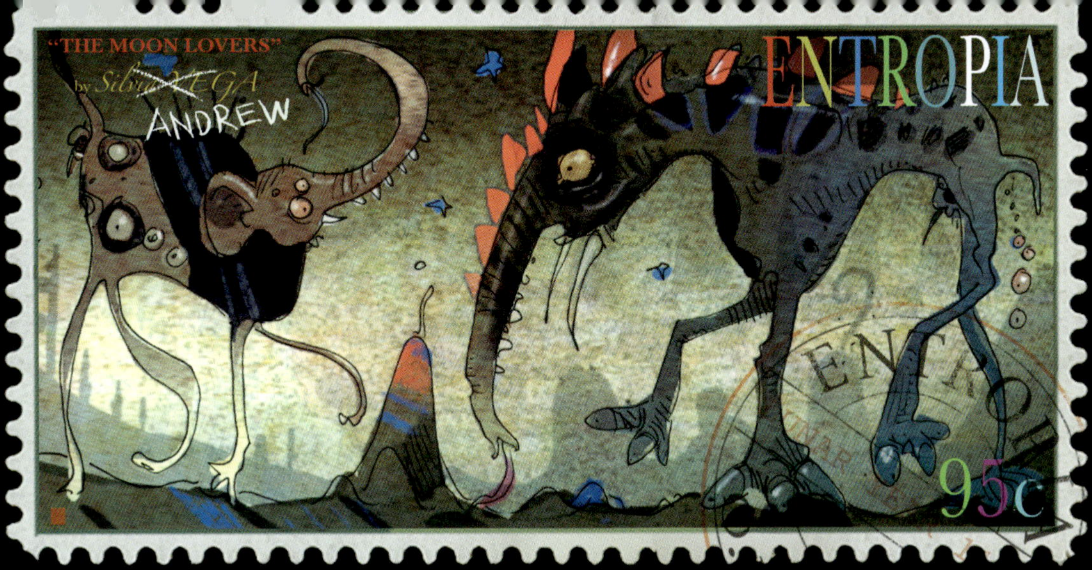

95c *The Moon Lovers*

APPRECIATION STAMP

For six consecutive years, the rabbits of Woodland Creek won all the skiing competitions held by the neighboring city of Ice Royale. One day, the infuriated coaches of the Ice Royale Ski Team decided to send a group of sports scientists and one anthropologist to Woodland Creek to find out what gave these rabbits their competitive edge. The group arrived at the rural village disguised as forest inspectors and started to secretly gather information about the rabbits' equipment and training methods and to investigate rumors of a possible miracle ski wax. After two weeks, the scientists were still clueless until anthropologist Dorothy Rouge made the first breakthrough. She befriended eight-time gold winner Blitz Speed, who disclosed to her that all the rabbit boys and girls learned skiing in the Wolf and Hunter survival camps, which were led by his grandfather Blitz Senior.

According to Speed, Blitz Senior accidentally invented downhill skiing as a youth while logging in upper Woodland Creek. As the story goes, he was cornered by a pack of wolves, backed up against a cliff with nowhere to go. In a moment of great lucidity, Senior tied two wood logs to his rabbit feet, dashed through the wolves' pack, and escaped the bewildered creatures with never-before-reached speed.

After telling this story, Speed then turned to the group's scientists and informed them that no expensive equipment or sophisticated training would lead their Ice Royale competitors to success. "We are winning," he said with a wink, "because we are skiing with our hearts, not our minds. You should give it a try."

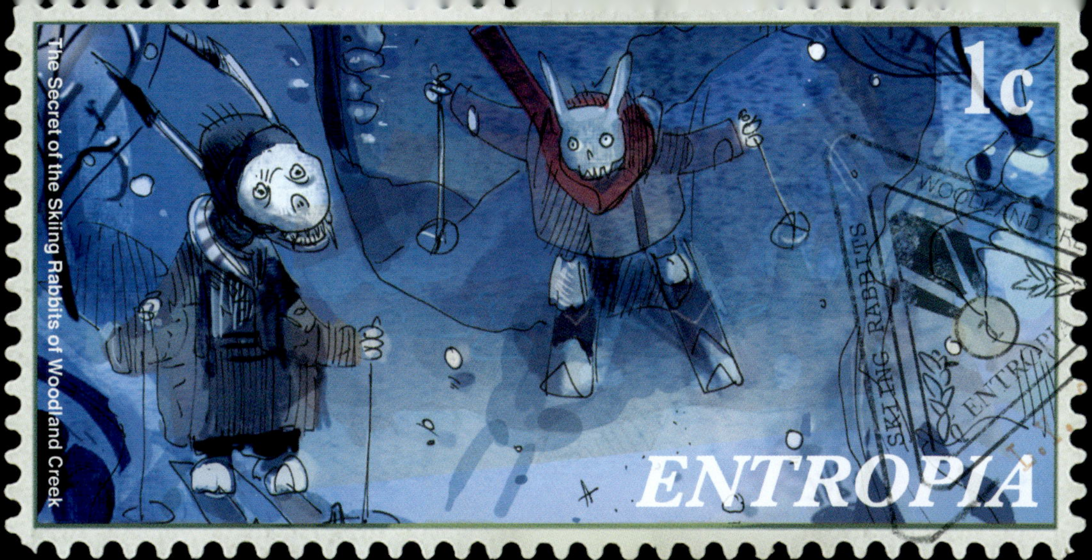

1c *The Secret of the Skiing Rabbits of Woodland Creek*

ACHIEVEMENT STAMP

On the third moon tide of lunar year 1001, Entropia City was ravaged by a flaming inferno caused by an inexplicable underground kitchen fire. In the ensuing chaos, a fireproof leader and his secret army staged a military coup, which ousted the Royal Entropian Family for nearly a decade.

The grueling years of the reign of the Childish Robot Czar and his Animatronic Army marked the darkest times in Entropian history.

The horrible poaching and warmongering came to an end when Queen Pingo the Young was able to take back her rightful throne and ban the Childish Robot Czar and his Animatronics to the magma island of Kundur.

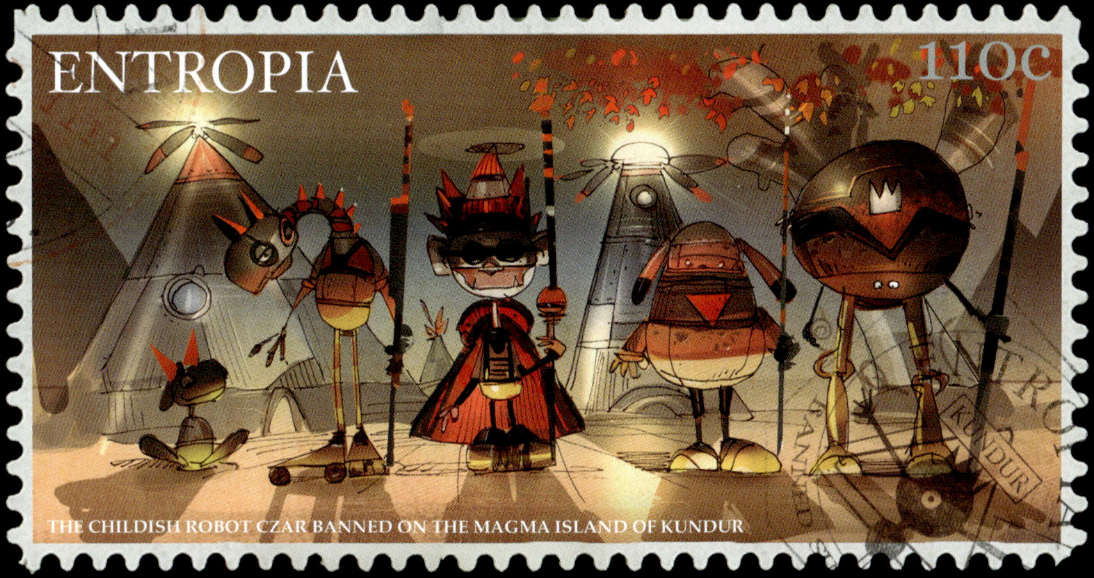

110C *The Childish Robot Czar and his Animatronics*

CARICATURE STAMP

Queen Pingo was 24, and the youngest member of the Royal Council, when for the first time she was able to introduce a bill that would grant equal rights to all sentient beings in Entropia. That was also the day when a devastating underground kitchen fire ravaged Entropia City and destroyed the royal palace.

The Childish Robot Czar and his Animatronic Shock Troops disguised themselves as royal firefighters, entered the burning city, and took power. When the Royal Council finally realized what had happened, it was too late. Pingo's family, Aunt Pongo and Uncle Eugenio, made it out of the burning city on the Moonshadow 4, while the local population smuggled Queen Pingo out of the city by train, disguising her as a flower girl, which earned her the nickname Entropia's Wild Rose.

For the next ten years, Queen Pingo lived in hiding all over Entropia, organizing the Resistance. Some believed that they saw her red biplane flying low through the night sky in the north, while others could have sworn that they recognized the Queen disguised as a naka-nut farmer in the south. But all of Entropia agreed that it was her distinctive voice they heard on the underground radio station Entropia Resist.

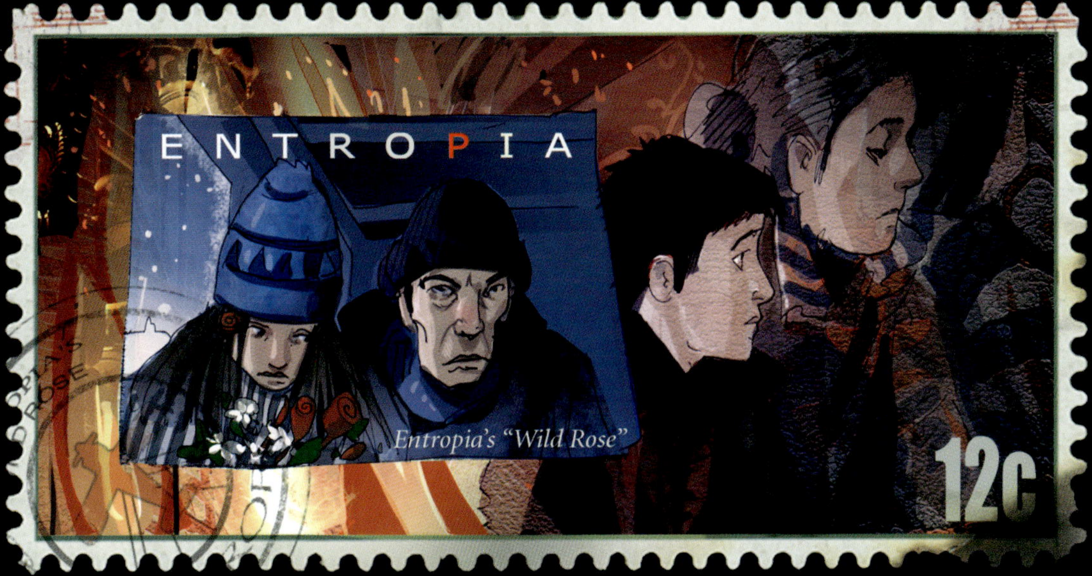

12c *Entropia's Wild Rose*

COMMEMORATIVE STAMP

An abundance of exotic plants and rare animals exist in Entropia's Jurassic plains of Murango. The place is best known, however, for a rare and precious type of sheep, whose wool of superb quality and iridescent color has fascinated Entropian tailors for centuries. Murango wool is produced by Murango sheep, which live freely in large flocks protected by highly aggressive guardian rams. Along with their unique wool, Murango sheep are most distinguished from their domesticated sheep cousins by their astonishing intellect. With an average IQ of 135, Murango sheep are one of the most intelligent sentient animals of Entropia.

The only way to obtain precious Murango wool is to appeal to a sheep's intellectual vanity by challenging it to a game of chess or Scrabble. If the challenger wins the game, the flock generally renounces the valuable wool. If the challenger loses, however, he or she has to remove their clothing and is likely to be chased while naked off the premises by the guardian rams.

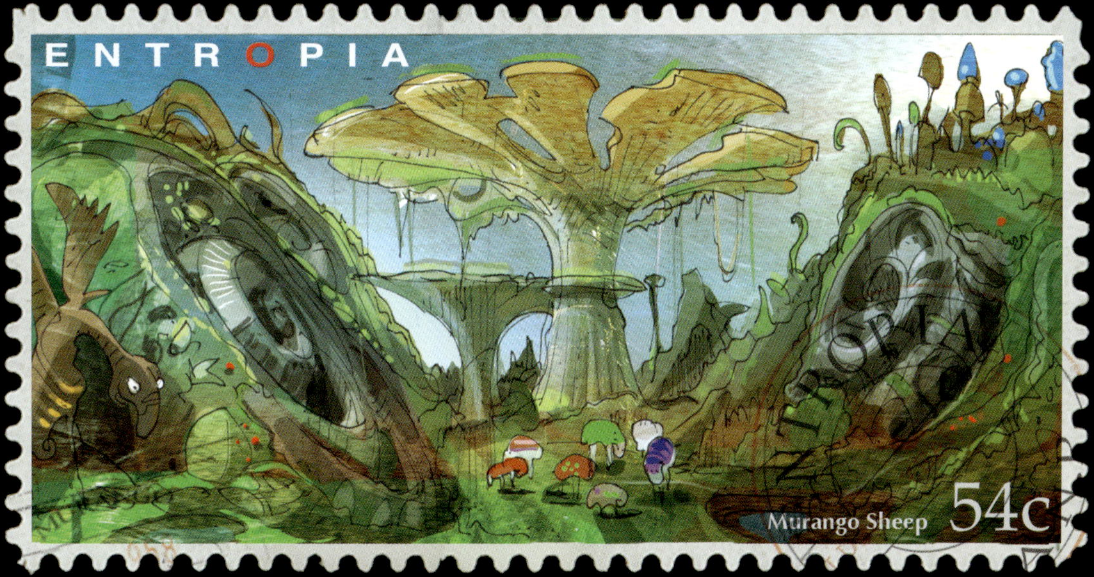

54c *Murango Sheep*

AGRICULTURAL STAMP

Teenage girls living in the fashionable, flying balloon-city Helium Nine could not get enough of small portable pets, which they carried in hopelessly overpriced backpacks and handbags.

Every week, flying merchants would arrive with new selections of Miniature Pigs and Dwarf Artwarks, until the craze culminated in the arrival of a strange species of Backpack Penguins that were able to sing the capital's latest opera hits. The problem with the singing Penguins became apparent when, after a day or two, the buyers realized that the only way to quiet them was to let them smoke an extremely expensive brand of cigarettes—which were also conveniently available from the flying merchants.

The singing Penguins became such a source of public distress that in lunar year 1012, Queen Pingo the Young declared them illegal. The poor creatures were returned to the Entropian Wildlife Society, which eventually came up with the solution of dropping them by parachute over the isolated magma islands of Kundur.

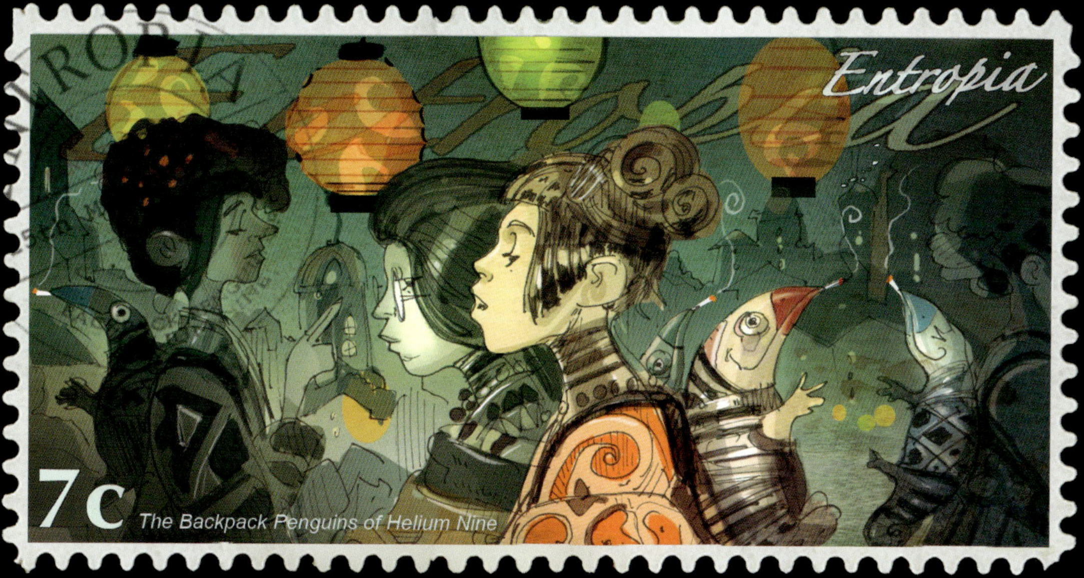

7c *The Backpack Penguins of Helium Nine*

PET-AWARENESS STAMP

During the Oceanic Conflict, under the reign of the Childish Robot Czar, Entropia entered an almost unstoppable arms race with the Independent Whale Cities of the Deep.

At its height, Entropia's Subnautical Fleet consisted of 400 submarines, also known as the Hunters of the Deep, and 350 armored ocean cruisers led by their flagship The Victory III. By the end of the war, over 6,000 sailors lost their lives in Entropia's coffins of steel.

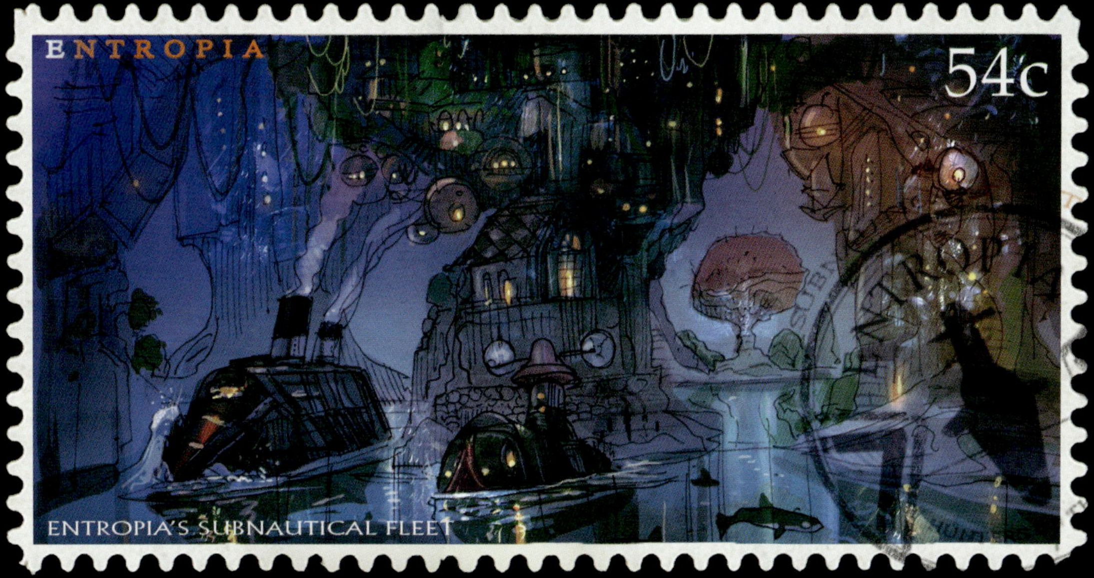

54c *Entropia's Subnautical Fleet*

WAR-PROPAGANDA STAMP

Entropians who have experienced a great loss or are suffering from severe stress can become melancholic or chronically depressed. Once the burden of sorrow becomes too heavy to carry, family members, friends, or even colleagues may appeal to the services of a Governmental Hope Whisperer.

For a small fee (often covered by Entropian health care), a Hope Whisperer visits the patients in their dreams and frees them of their sadness and emotional burden, so they can awaken refreshed and hopeful the next day.

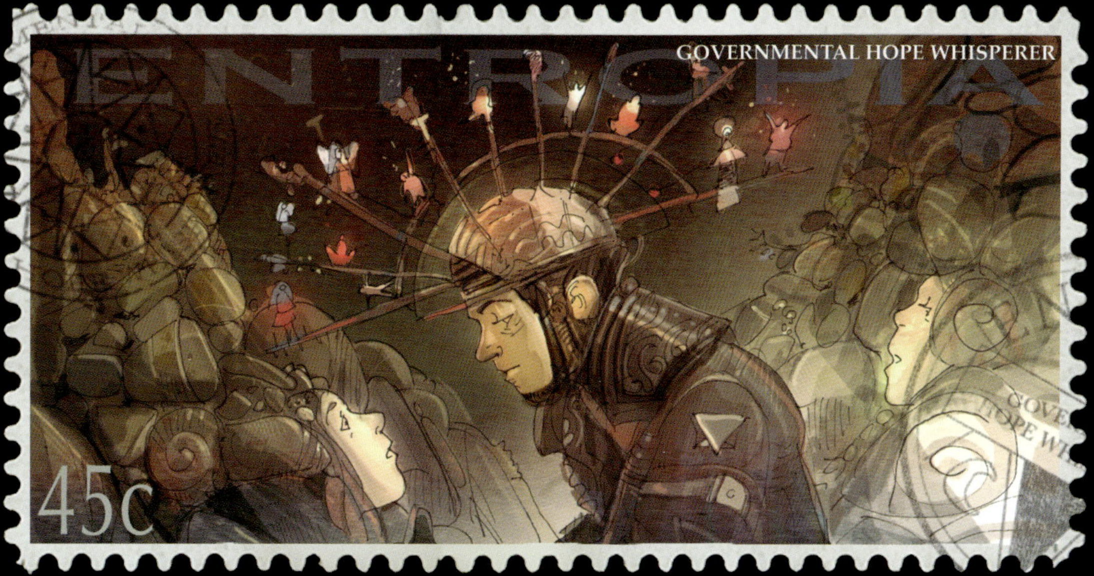

45C *Governmental Hope Whisperer*

HEALTH-ADVISORY STAMP

Marquis de Salade, with his signature wig made from fresh romaine lettuce, is considered one of the most controversial figures in Entropia's history.

At 35, he spent half of his massive inheritance on a string of exuberant celebrations in his own honor and architectural endeavors of regrettable taste. In his eccentric decadence, he was known to be a negligent master of estate and his staff of 900 (basically the entire population of Black Pebble River) neither loved nor respected him. To illustrate, a children's song of the time features the line, "Salad head with a heart of lead, leave us alone, we wish you were dead."

During the war years, however, he redeemed himself by hiding hundreds of farmers and their children in the citadels of his castle. In doing so, he saved them from being deported to work in the agonizing Machine Cities of the Childish Robot Czar.

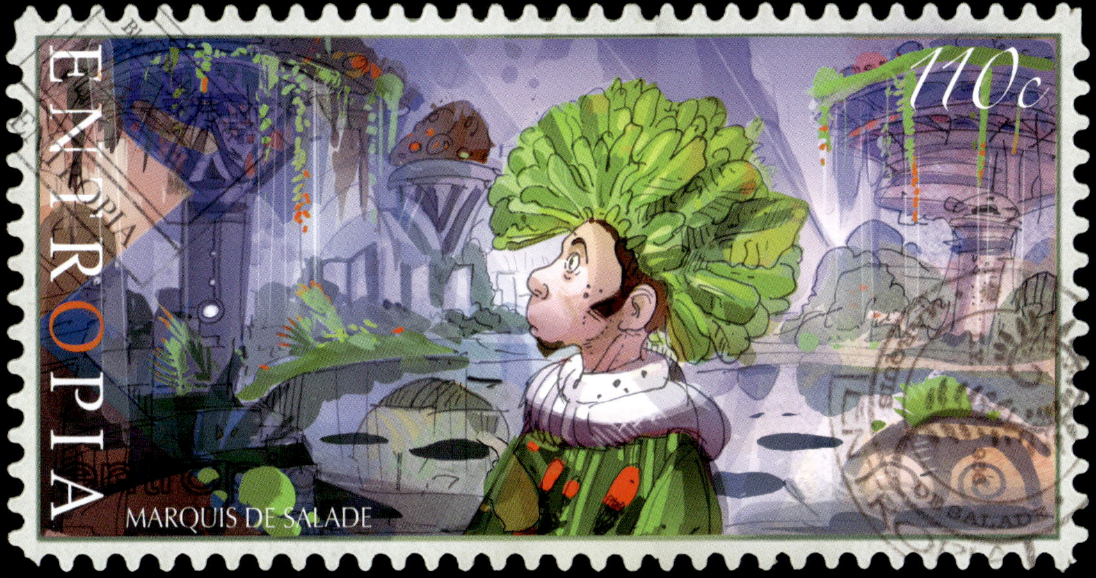

110c *Marquis de Salade*

COMMEMORATIVE STAMP

It is well-documented that the citizens of Entropia are crazy about their pets and would never travel without them. Toward the end of the century, traveling by airships equipped with safe helium gas became the most fashionable pastime for the Entropian upper crust. That is, until lunar year 963 when Moon Shadow 1, the largest airship of Entropia's air fleet, nearly plunged into the Northern Sea's icy water due to rapid loss of gas pressure combined with decreased maneuverability.

The catastrophe was averted by first-class mechanic Valerie Ping, who was able to quickly repair the damage. Her accident report stated that the damage was started by two pet ferrets, which apparently escaped from their owners on previous flights. In their confusion, the ferrets chewed through the main gas lines and steering cables. The delinquent animals were returned to their rightful owners, who apologized profusely for the trouble caused by their impetuous pets.

Since this incident, however, pet transport is only allowable in specially designed travel bags. Protesting what they viewed as the discriminatory treatment of their beloved animals, Entropian bourgeoisie decided to travel exclusively by cruise ship or, if absolutely necessary, by luxury train.

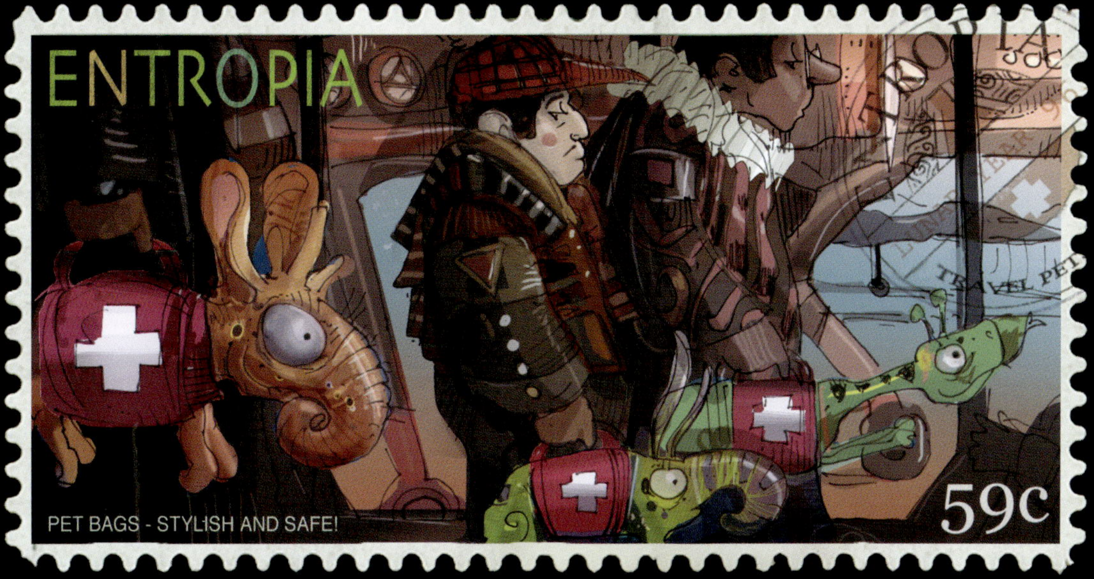

59c *Traveling Pets*

PET-AWARENESS STAMP

"Does your teenager partake in slumber parties on your local cemetery accompanied by new somberly cloaked friends? Has your darling pet parrot been traded in for a gaunt black crow? Are your youngster's grades a searing disappointment and will no university allow he or she to matriculate? There is still one last hope: Place your sons or daughters in the Institute for the Occult and Bizarre (I.F.O.B.) where they can safely study astrology, alchemy, and parapsychology on our highly equipped campus in the medieval town of Kandinsk."

This ad or ones similar to it were found in newspapers all around Entropia when the first private school for the occult and bizarre opened in lunar year 945. The school became a great success despite some initial setbacks such as the frequent burning down of the alchemy wing. Many graduates found satisfying careers in the nearby city of Kukursk as certified fortune-tellers, mind readers, and magnetologists, taking their place among the many emerging professions in the magic sector.

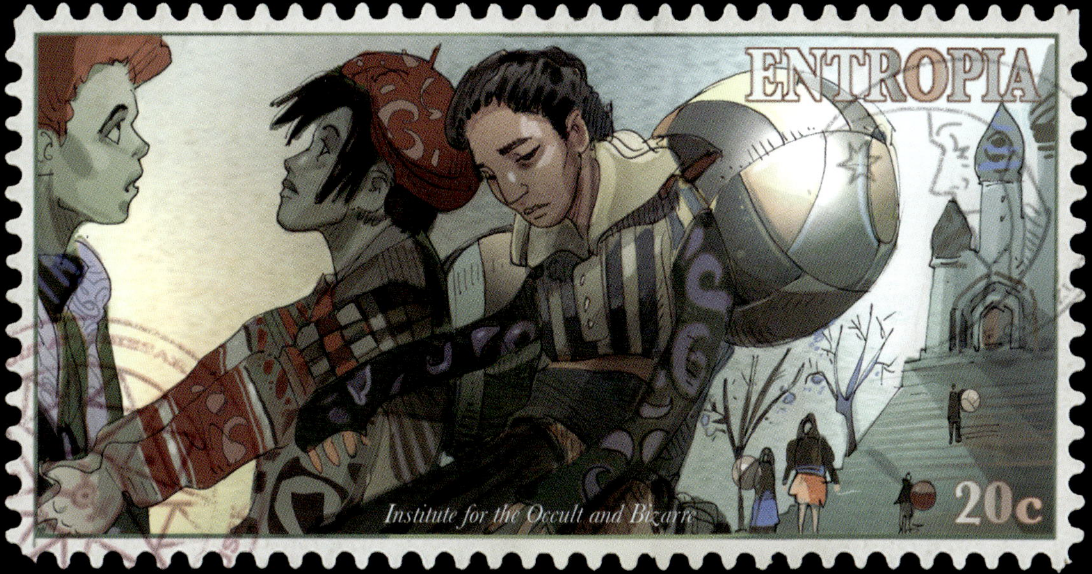

20c *Institute for the Occult and Bizarre*

PROMOTIONAL STAMP

Entropian historians don't agree on the origin of the double-headed monuments that are found in many of the rivers in the northern territories of Entropia. Some believe that a pre-Entropian civilization erected them to pacify the river gods, while others speculate that a clan of ancient Axolotls built them long before they returned to the ocean.

The only fact that is known for certain is that the monuments make for discreet meeting places where young Entropian couples go to play the highly popular game Together Alone.

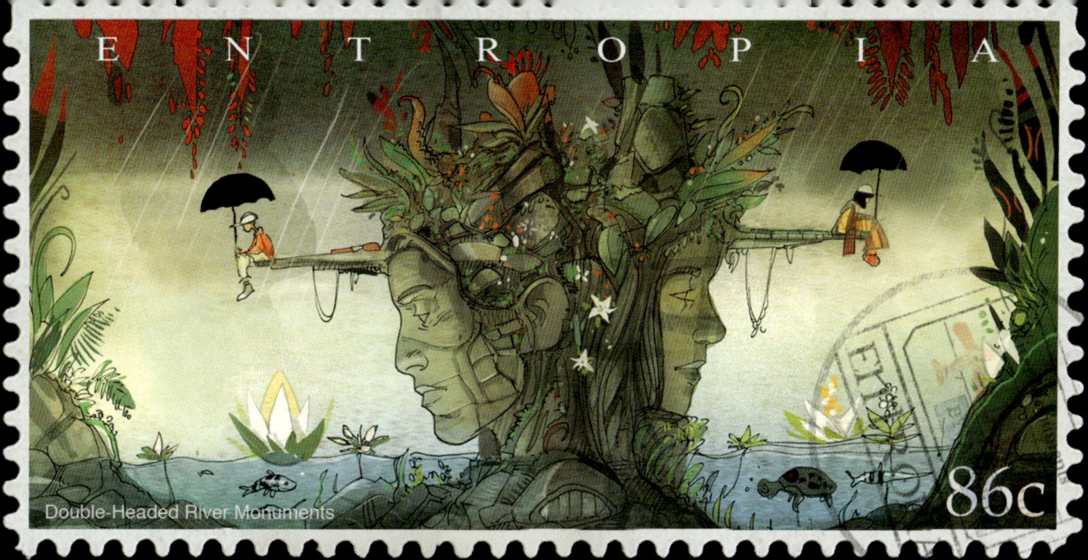

86c *Double-Headed River Monuments*

HISTORICAL CONSERVATION STAMP

On the inhospitable ice islands of the north live the mysterious Egg-rolling Women of Polaris. Due to their remote location, this Eskimo tribe stayed undiscovered until just recently, when Sir Allen Mackenzie met them by accident on his expedition to study the mating behavior of the gray-spotted snow weasel.

Here is an excerpt from his expedition diary:

"Day 165

Having traveled 500 miles along the snowy coast of Polaris, my faithful snow dogs and I were at the end of our resources and still no snow weasel in sight. Is this expedition doomed? I wondered, when I suddenly spotted a group of Eskimo women singing and dancing on the snowy ocean shore in the moonlight. I took cover in the powdery snow and observed the strange scene. What happened next was so outrageous that I had a hard time believing my partially snow-blind eyes. A sea turtle of gargantuan proportions emerged out of the ocean and crawled up to the group of little women, who promptly surrounded the massive head of the heavily breathing creature and began hugging and kissing it. The turtle then laid nine huge eggs in the soft snow and returned to the sea. The youngest women turned to roll the eggs up the hill toward what appeared to be a group of preprepared breeding igloos. The next day, I was spotted by an Eskimo girl who brought me to her clan leader. In the ceremonial igloo, I learned that the women have a secret agreement with the giant turtle—the Grandmother of the Sea. In return for protecting her eggs from the snow weasels, which I have yet to encounter, the giant sea turtle protects the tribe's sons and husbands who venture by kayak in the summer months to provide food for the winter."

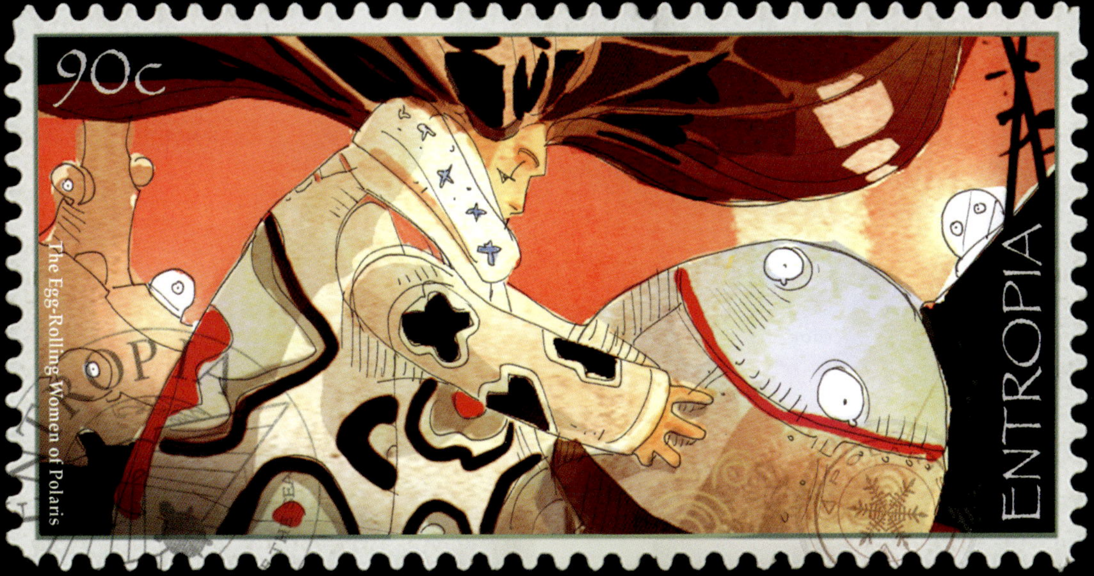

90c *The Egg-Rolling Women of Polaris*

EXPLORATION STAMP

Shortly after the Childish Robot Czar took power, he ordered the intensive hunt of the protected Wilderwhales. This caused increasing tension with the populations of the free Axolotl reef cities and culminated in the accidental sinking of the Czar's whale-poaching fleet in the Bay of Takashiro. For revenge, the Childish Robot Czar and his Animatronic Shock Troops launched a furious attack on the free Axolotl reef cities, officially starting the ten-year Oceanic Wars. The peaceful Axolotls were forced to evacuate their majestic underwater dwellings and vanished out of sight to a secret location in the Entropian Sea's uncharted parts.

For ten years, the Czar's Subnautical Fleet tried in vain to find the secret base from which mysterious Orca Rebels launched an aquatic guerrilla war on those who dared to travel by sea. Later, it was discovered that the Axolotls and the Wilderwhales had created a symbiotic pact in which the Masterwhales allowed the Axolotls to build their cities on their backs. The Axolotls, in return, created mobile krill harvest stations and orca patrols, thus saving the whales and themselves from sure extinction by the Czar and his Subnautical Fleet.

In lunar year 1016, Queen Pingo the Young was the first and only Entropian to be allowed to visit the Whale Cities of the Deep. She told her great grandchildren stories about the beautiful underwater cities but never disclosed their location to anyone.

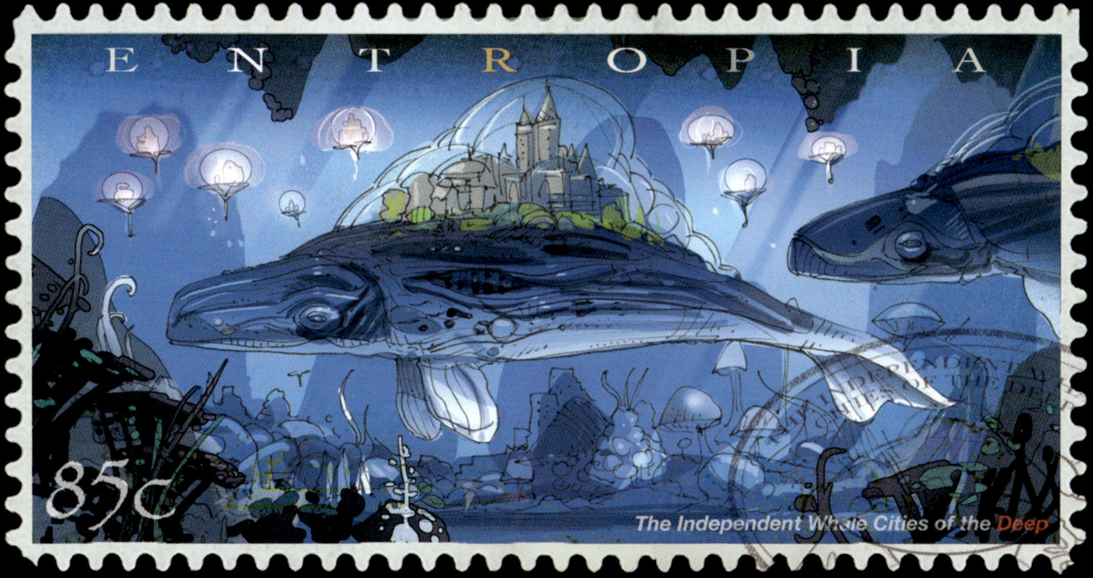

85c The Independent Whale Cities of the Deep

COMMEMORATIVE STAMP

For over half a century, the astronomers of Kukursk predicted the arrival of a great solar eclipse and all the bad luck and misfortune that would accompany it. When darkness finally set in, nine years after the astronomers' prediction, light disappeared quickly and didn't return for a month. Much of the terrified population believed the sun would never return and that the end of their planet was near. Looking for a culprit for the calamity, a group of concerned Kukursk citizens had the astronomers unofficially arrested and locked up in the town's observatory. They decided that the astronomers would not be released until they found the lost sun and brought it back again.

For the next few weeks, pandemonium reigned in Entropia. Wolves were reported in the cities, and ghostly packs of nocturnal fishrats ascended from the sewer systems, adding to the chaos.

When the sun returned as unexpectedly as it disappeared, the astronomers were released and celebrated as national heroes.

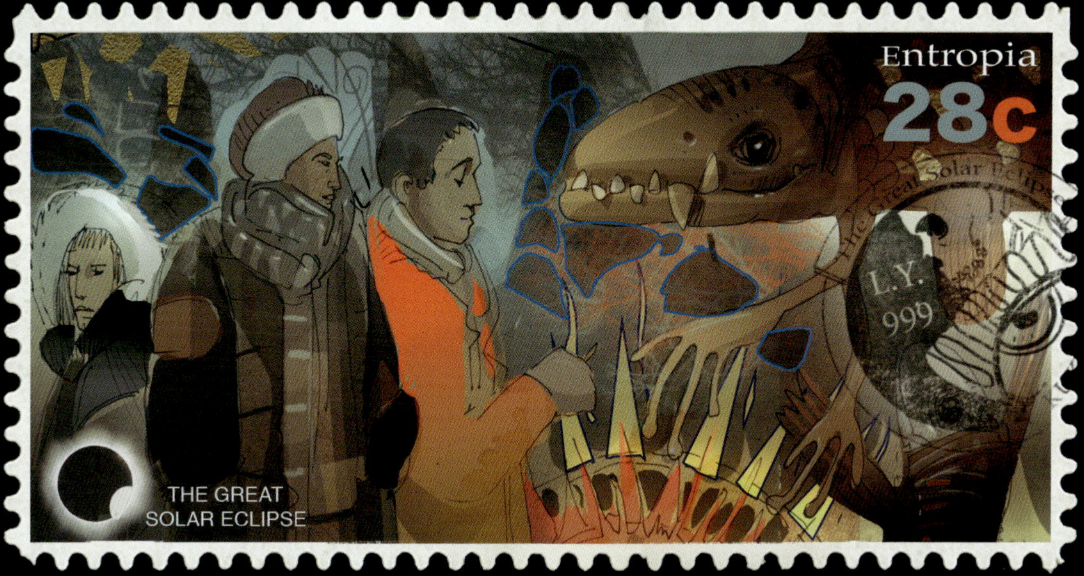

28c *The Great Solar Eclipse*

COMMEMORATIVE STAMP

During the ten-year reign of the Childish Robot Czar and his Animatronics, a large portion of Entropia's population was forced to work in the weapons factories of the new Machine Cities. Toward the war's end, pollution reached such extreme levels that the Czar ordered the mandatory wearing of governmental gas masks, which were distributed and enforced by his Animatronic Shock Troops.

The gas masks, or "Filter Beaks" as Entropians called them, were ridiculously uncomfortable and made it hard to breathe, see, hear, eat and absolutely impossible to speak.

Most Entropians knew that the Childish Robot Czar never cared about their health. The awkwardly designed masks had only one real purpose: to effectively silence the steadily increasing voices of dissent.

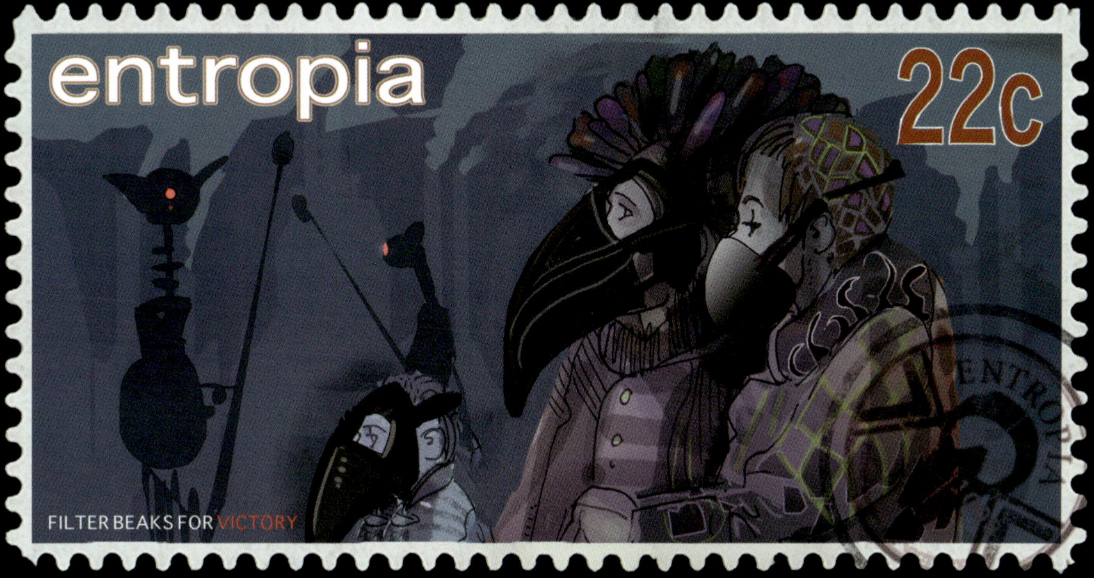

22c *Filter Beaks for Victory*

WAR-PROPAGANDA STAMP

The Obsidian Brotherhood was an occult group of Entropian alchemists and architects who were promised fortunes by the Childish Robot Czar if they participated in the war effort and designed the weapon-producing Machine Cities. In order to keep their identities secret and to protect their families from the repercussions of disgruntled Entropian citizens, the group agreed to wear black gowns and robotic masks provided by the Czar's Animatronic Surgeon. What the Czar failed to disclose was that the masks, once fitted, could only be removed when the group's contracts were fulfilled and the gigantic Machine Cities completed.

Survivors of this time testify that the "Architects of the Dark" could often be seen late at night, roaming the metal streets and corridors, gesticulating over blueprints, and scanning construction sites with their robotic eyes. As time went by, the masked collaborators, while feverishly trying to finish their never-ending assignments, came to realize that the robotic masks would never be removed. Many of them lost their minds, and one escaped into the tropical rain forest of Akahui, where he was worshipped as a lost god by a confused indigenous tribe.

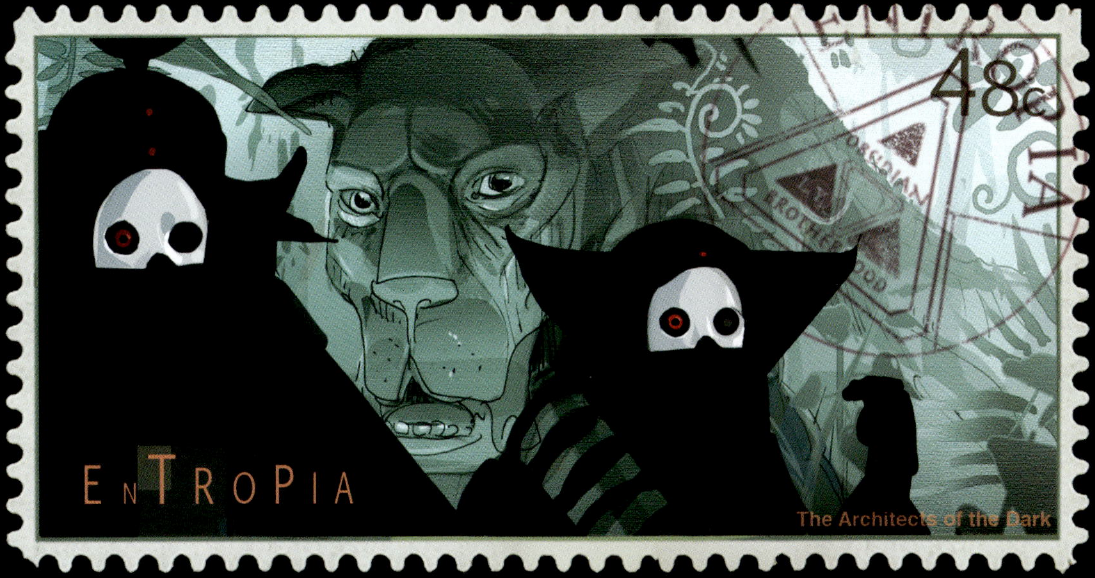

48c *The Architects of the Dark*

WAR-PROPAGANDA STAMP

It was the young Axolotl Viceroy Akar of the Independent Whale Cities who altered the path of history by offering a truce to end the ten-year Oceanic Wars.

Against the will of his elders, Akar secretly met with Queen Pingo the Young on the armored ocean-cruiser Victory III. The peace agreement they devised granted safe ocean passage for all Entropians, who in return would discontinue the hunting of the Wilderwhales and all sentient ocean creatures.

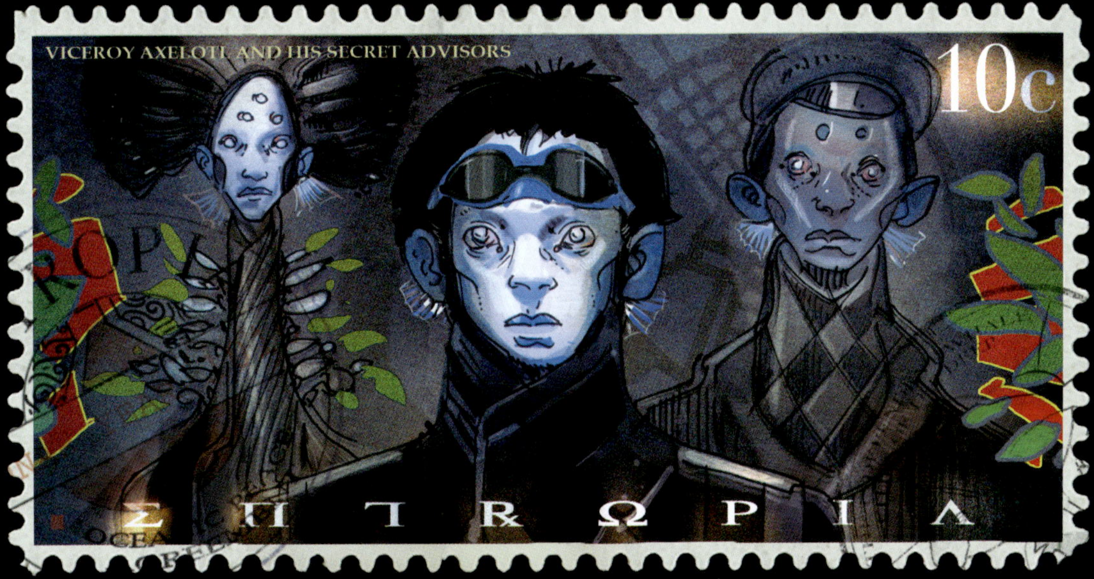

10c *The Oceanic Peace Agreement*

COMMEMORATIVE STAMP

The northeastern city of Kukursk used to be known as the Healing Light of the North. It is located directly on the Entropian North Pole, which predestined it to become a center for electromagnetic therapies. Despite the fact that the Entropian Medical Association continually refused to acknowledge the therapeutic electromagnetic powers of the city's location, thousands of patients made an annual pilgrimage to Kukursk by snowrail or reindeer sled to enjoy the healing effects of the city, with its magnetic baths, magnet stone massage therapies, and souvenirs in the form of magnetic pendulums or bracelets.

During one particularly grim winter, a strange event occurred that changed Kukursk's destiny forever. On New Year's Eve of lunar year 1005, a group of children witnessed an enormous cloud moving slowly toward the city center and prepared for yet another snowstorm. What the children first thought was snow descending from the sky turned out to be a huge flock of floating miniature cows. No one—not the zoologists of the Entropian Wildlife Society nor the doctors of the Entropian Medical Association—could explain where the cows came from, why they were so small in size, and, most importantly, why they were able to float. After months of fruitless research, they concurred that the Minicows were harmless, and for the first time they officially acknowledged the city's magnetic powers.

Kukursk's citizens did not care about the scientists' and doctors' findings, since the small, gentle cows turned out to be an even bigger tourist attraction. Thereafter, magnetic souvenir salesmen dropped their wares in favor of restorative and nutritious minicow milk, minicow cheese, and good-luck minicow charm bracelets.

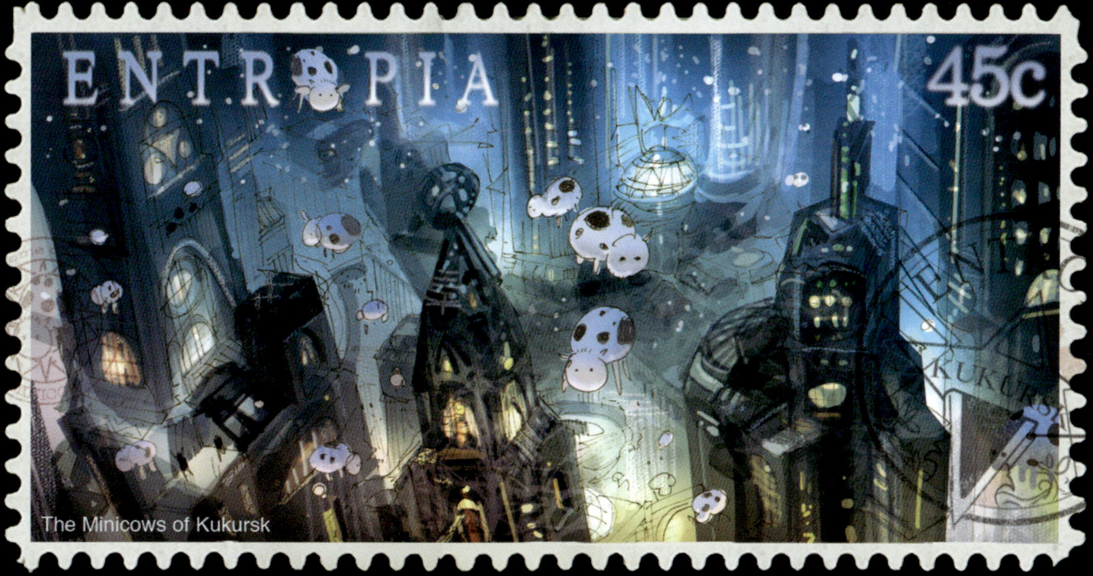

45c *The Minicows of Kukursk*

PROMOTIONAL STAMP

In the Entropian heartland lays the ancient Fungus Sanctuary, which is surrounded by an almost impenetrable swamp. Due to its great number of poisonous mushrooms, the sanctuary has always been dangerous and foolish to enter. Over time, however, outcasts and people persecuted by the law have sought asylum in the million-year-old refuge. Under the rule of the Childish Robot Czar, the Fungus Sanctuary became home for Entropia's dissidents and refugees. Here, persecuted farmers, artists, scientists, and nobles hid from the Animatronic Shock Troops and made plans to take back their country.

A scientist who refused to collaborate with the Czar's Animatronic war scientists arrived at the forest with his family and discovered that the spores of an insignificant-looking mushroom had the ability to penetrate even the strongest Animatronic armor and paralyze Animatronic circuitry. This information made it to Queen Pingo, who was leading the Resistance and hiding in the highlands disguised as a naka farmer. Under her brilliant leadership, seeds from the mysterious mushroom were smuggled into all Machine Cities and in every town and village of Entropia. On M-Day (Mushroom Day), underground radio stations played the song "Mushroom Soup–It's Good For You," thereby signaling the Resistance to plant the fast-growing mushroom seeds. During the following week, mushroom spores effectively paralyzed the Animatronic armies and factories, and the people of Entropia were finally able to put an end to robotic occupation.

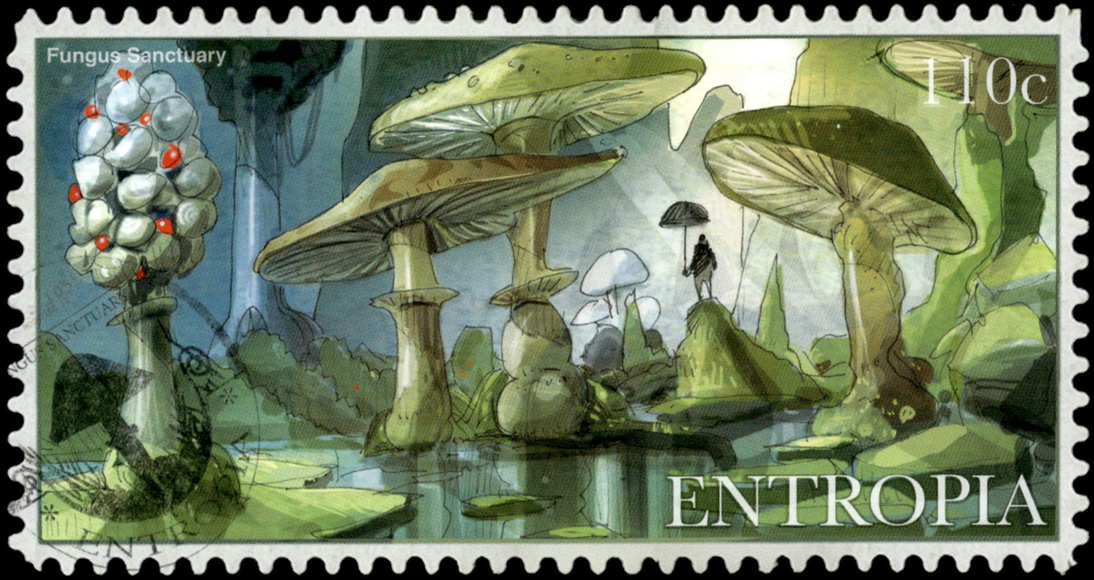

110c *The Fungus Sanctuary*

COMMEMORATIVE STAMP

In lunar year 1011, Entropia's inhabitants ended the occupation put in place by the Childish Robot Czar and his Animatronic Shock Troops. Queen Pingo returned to the capital and in an inspiring speech publicly renounced her crown. With this bold move, the Queen turned Entropia into the first direct democracy. The new Entropian council included representatives from all the sentient beings of the nation.

Former Queen Pingo was elected president of the council in an overwhelming majority and stayed in office for the next eight years. Uncle Eugenio became Cultural Ambassador and Aunt Pongo was elected Educational Minister. In the years to follow, Pongo succeeded in revolutionizing Entropia's school system. Child labor was abolished and all of Entropia's children were granted the right to obtain an education.

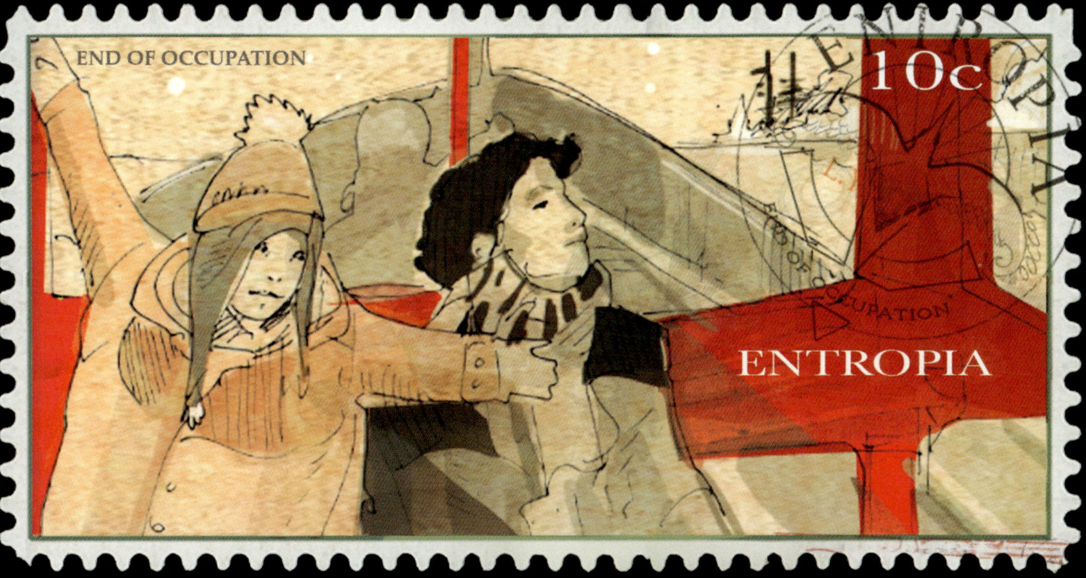

10c *End of Occupation*
JUBILATION STAMP

At the end of the Oceanic Conflict, the war-torn southern provinces of Alkaleb and Sunora were hit by a devastating drought. Upon regaining her rightful throne and ousting the Childish Robot Czar, Queen Pingo the Young spontaneously launched a relief operation to help the people of the south.

What started with a caravan of ten vehicles filled with grain and medical supplies in Entropia City grew, under Queen Pingo's charismatic leadership, into the biggest relief operation ever launched. In every province the caravan crossed, more vehicles filled with lifesaving goods were entered into the race to save the starving populations of Alkaleb and Sunora. When the caravan finally arrived in Sunora, led by Queen Pingo in her trusty single-engine biplane, it was over 1,000 vehicles strong.

Today Alkaleb and Sunora are thriving desert cities. Nothing remains of the hardship once endured except an annual friendship rally that starts in Entropia City and ends in Sunora, commemorating what is referred to in Entropian history books as the Great Race.

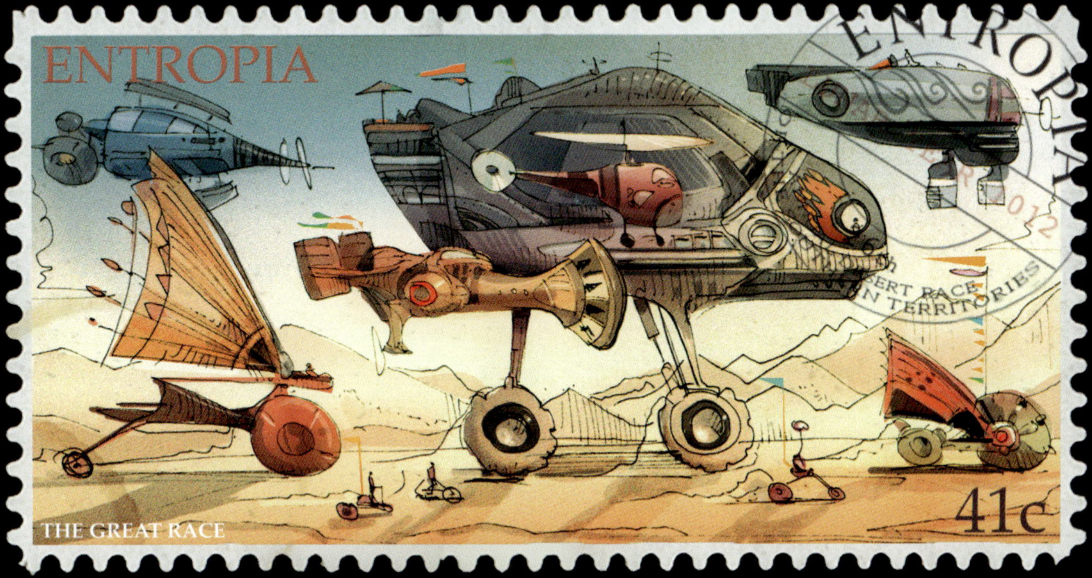

41c *The Great Race*

COMMEMORATIVE STAMP

At the end of the ten-year Oceanic Wars, a truce was made between the Axolotls of the Independent Whale Cities and the dry-land Entropians. To celebrate the newfound peace, the Axolotls granted Entropia the right to build an underwater railroad, connecting for the first time in history the northern and southern territories of Entropia.

Initially the Aquarail was met with a considerable amount of suspicion by the Entropians, but gained increasing popularity thanks to very inexpensive Aquarail passes for students and seniors.

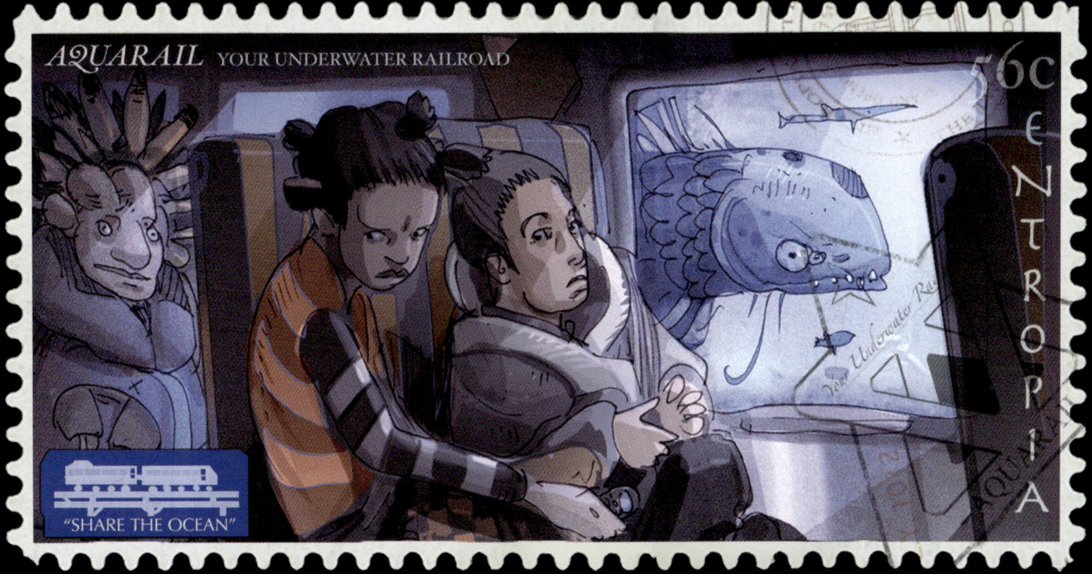

56c *AquaRail: Your Underwater Railroad*

PROMOTIONAL STAMP

All of Entropia fell in love with the adorable miniature cows that one day miraculously landed in Kukursk. Thousands of tourists flocked to the city on the newly established airship connection, Minicow Express to see the small creatures. It was considered chic to rent a Minicow on a leash, stroll down the boulevards, and sample Minicow products such as Minimilk, Minicheese, and Minichocolate, which were sold all over town. The famous artist couple Gloria and Jean-Paul stated that Minicow milk altered their artistic perception, and as a result prices of their Minicow paintings started to soar.

On the opening of their new show, entitled "***The Minicow Speaks to Me***," the artists themselves became the first fatalities linked to Minicows. Surrounded by hundreds of gala guests marveling over their newest paintings, Gloria and Jean-Paul jumped hand in hand from the forty-ninth floor of the Kukursk Luxury Towers while singing the opera hit "Volare." Over the next few weeks, more and more people, believing that they could fly, jumped from buildings to their death, often while singing. Alarmed Entropian scientists concurred that the mysterious disease (*dementia Volare-cantare*) was clearly linked to the consumption of Minimilk products, which were immediately removed from the shelves of specialty stores throughout Entropia.

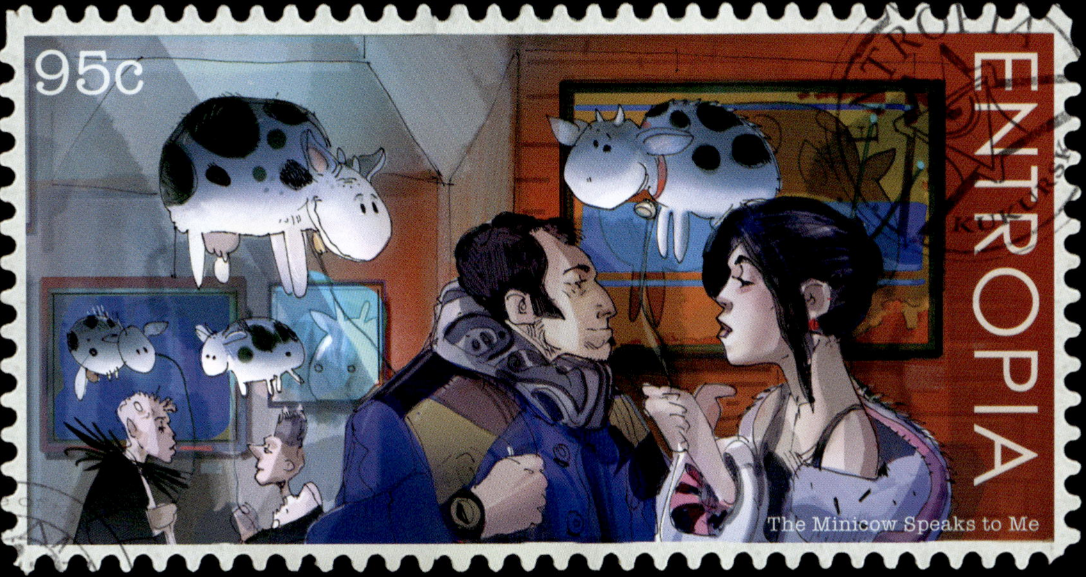

95c *The Minicow Speaks to Me*

HEALTH-AWARENESS STAMP

Gorgonzola Fischer, also known as the Living Christmas Tree, and his partner Mark Snyder, the Human Torch, are considered the most influential entertainers of greater Entropia.

They met as young men on the cruise ship Equinox II, where young Gorgonzola was performing a dismal magic show that featured a single domesticated fire lemur. At the time, Mark was trying his luck, in vain, as a celebrity impersonator. One fateful December night, while Gorgonzola was decorating his Christmas tree, his fire lemur Mandalai escaped from his cage and found his way to the main stage, where Mark was performing to an increasingly disinterested audience. Gorgonzola arrived on stage, Christmas tree in hand, trying to gain control of the escaped lemur and accidentally set Mark's highly flammable hairpiece on fire. To the surprise of both performers, the audience believed that the whole incident was part of the act and burst out in a roaring applause.

The following day, the two entertainers decided to create a joint act called Gorgonzola and Mark's Fantasy Fire Show. The show evolved into the biggest variety attraction Entropia had ever witnessed, featuring up to 180 fire lemurs, a captured Wilderbeast, and guest artists from all over the continent. All that remains from the original show is its climax, when a man disguised as a Christmas tree "accidentally" lights a celebrity impersonator on fire.

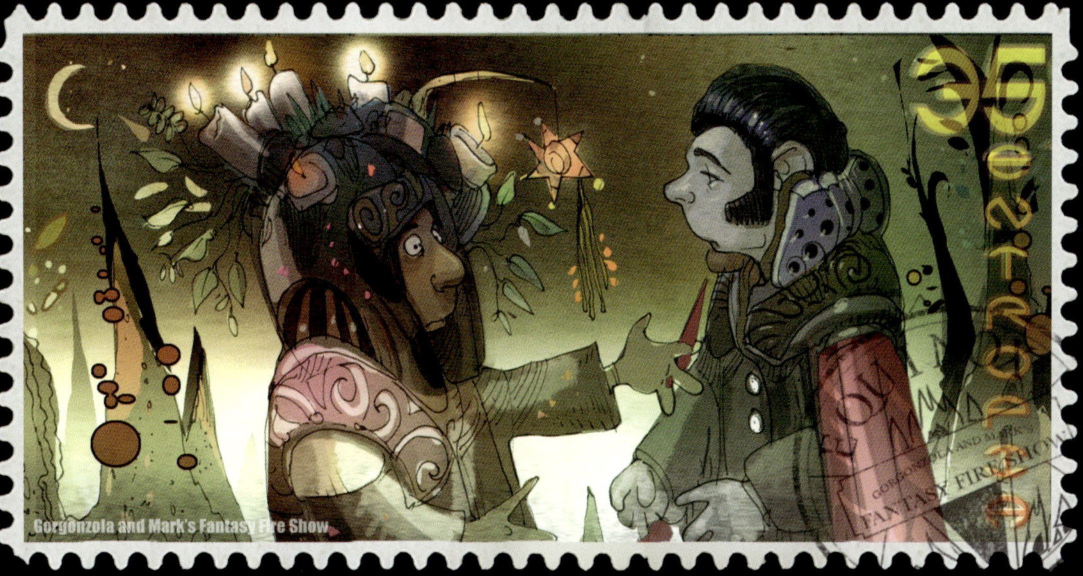

35c *Gorgonzola and Mark's Fantasy Fire Show*

FRIENDSHIP STAMP

Night after night, the same eerie spectacle unfolds in the vehicle-free city of Somnabul. As soon as the sun goes down, Somnabul's streets fill with thousands of sleepwalkers and tourists, roaming the cobblestone streets, coffeehouses, museums, and parks. In the early morning hours, they return quietly to homes and hotels where they wake up in their beds with absolutely no memories at all of their nightly adventures.

In earlier times, the sleepwalkers caused horrible traffic jams and endless confusion. Fortunately, things changed for the better when Queen Pingo the Young declared Somnabul a completely traffic-free zone and sleep tourism started to boom. Nowadays, thousands of tourists flock to Somnabul every year to either watch the nightly spectacle or to go on sleepwalks themselves in the colorful pajamas and glowing warning hats provided by hotels and sleep sanatoriums.

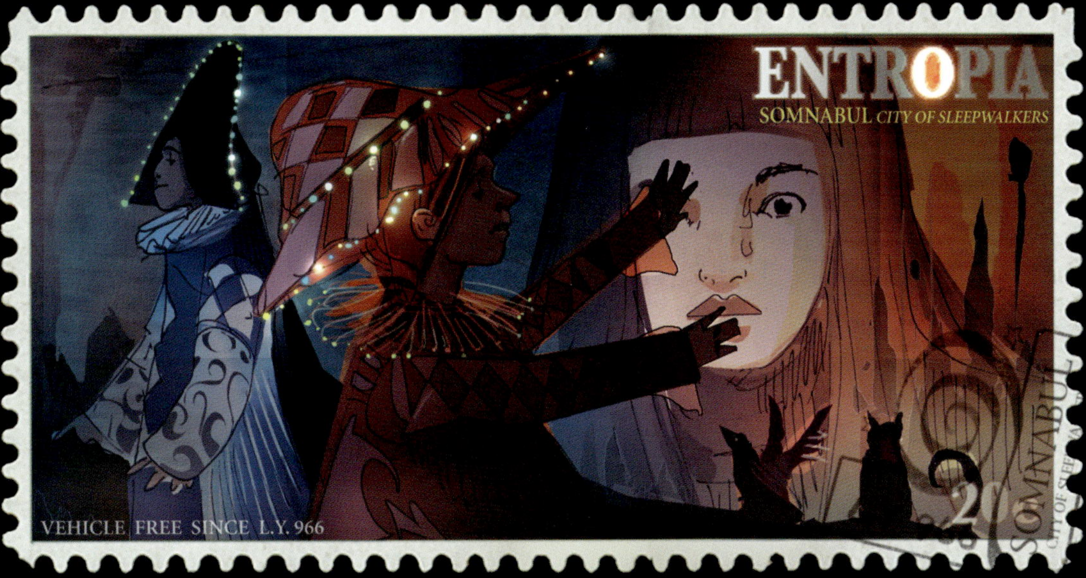

20c *Somnabul: City of Sleepwalkers*

PROMOTIONAL STAMP

Every autumn, an enormous flock of migrating parrots lands on Ice Royale's frozen lakes to gather strength and stamina for their annual migration from Kundur's magma islands to Akahui's tropical rain forest.

Ice Royale citizens used to love the colorful spectacle, feeding the parrots white naka nuts and marveling at their ability to mimic human speech. In the last ten years, however, the parrots have begun to utter statements such as "Down with the royal family!" "Long live the Czar," and a string of profanities that should not be repeated. It is worth noting that the parrots' use of foul language coincides with the banning of the Childish Robot Czar and his Animatronics to the Magma Islands of Kundur, where the migrating parrots spend their summers.

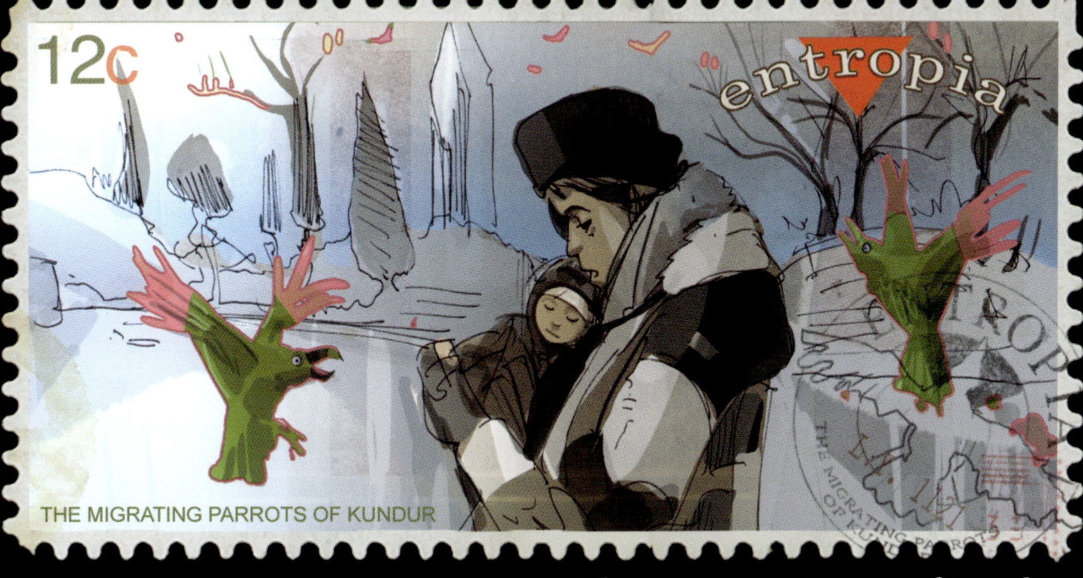

12c *The Migrating Parrots of Kundur*

NATURE STAMP

For years, the archeologist Professor Von Blister maintained his hypothesis that oversized humans once roamed the lands of Entropia. His controversial theory gained momentum when he excavated an eight-foot-long artifact in the high plateaus of Murango that he estimated was a petrified toothbrush for giants.

In lunar year 951, his theory was finally confirmed when a group of royal botanists accidentally discovered two perfectly preserved petrified giants in Entropia's inland swamps. In Professor Von Blister's book ***The Bathing Giants***, he explains that millions of years ago the Entropian swamps were tar pits. According to Von Blister, the male and female giants, which he lovingly named Trudy and Harvie, probably ventured into the pits to take a ritual mud bath and then became unconscious from the sulfuric gases, dying in their sleep.

For the rest of his life, Professor Von Blister tried in vain to raise funds to excavate and move the giants to Entropia's Museum of Natural History. Today the giants are almost forgotten, except upon occasion by a group of mysterious visitors passing through en route to the Fungus Sanctuary.

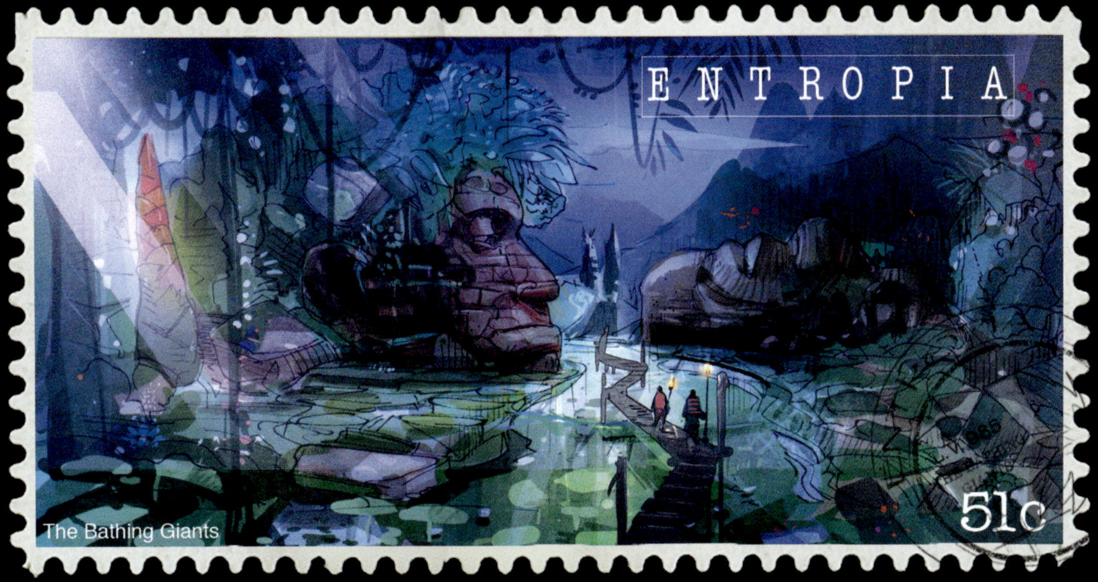

51c *The Bathing Giants*
CONSERVATION STAMP

In the lowlands of Thaa there exists a popular legend of an enormous Rabbitman that was in love with a young village maiden. He loved her so much that he created a beautiful fruit orchard filled with delicious grapes and apricots. The young woman also liked the giant Rabbitman, but her parents deemed the romance impossible because of their blatant difference in size and because of the rabbit's tremendous weight. When the Rabbitman asked for the hand of their daughter, the parents sadly stated, "We are not comfortable marrying our daughter off to a 400-pound rabbit, and that's final."

The rejected Rabbitman didn't take the news lightly. In a blind rage, he started to destroy the beautiful orchard, ripping out the vines and trampling the fruit. After a daylong rampage, he collapsed on his back, lamenting his weight. When night fell, he began to compulsively eat the fermenting fruit that surrounded him and then drifted into a soothing slumber.

It was noted by Thaa's citizens that over the next year, the Rabbitman started to experiment with fermented fruit and in the process invented winemaking. Today, Thaa boasts some of the finest wineries in Entropia.

There is little remaining of the legend of the giant Rabbitman and the maiden, with the exception of an excellent Thaa red wine called Pinot di Lapino.

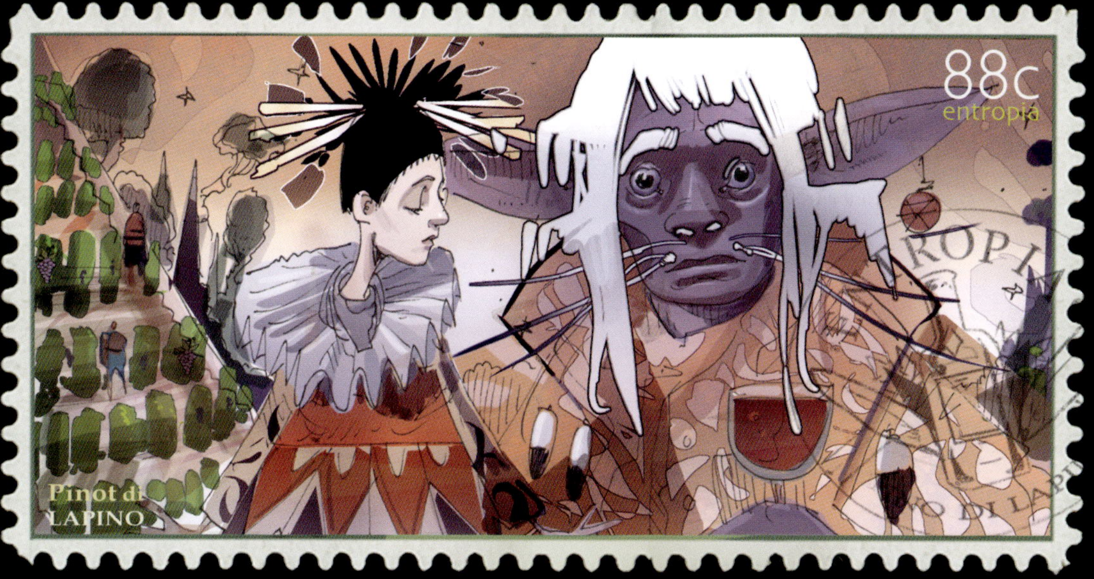

88c *Pinot di Lapino*

PROMOTIONAL STAMP

A large number of Entropians follow the 2,000-year-old teachings of the dream monk Xiu the Third. Disciples of his school of thought believe that upon death the deceased travel on the back of a ruby-red eel to the World of Perpetual Dreaming. Before the long journey begins, however, they first arrive at an underground lake where the eel kindly asks them to return their bodies, faces, and memories for recycling.

It is said that the only things the faceless travelers are allowed to take with them from their old existence are the clothes upon their backs. This is why Xiu-Entropians are often buried in their best suits and special burial scarves, within which are woven unique patterns representing the deceased's name, family crests, and milestones of their lives. The longer the Entropian lives, the longer the burial scarf.

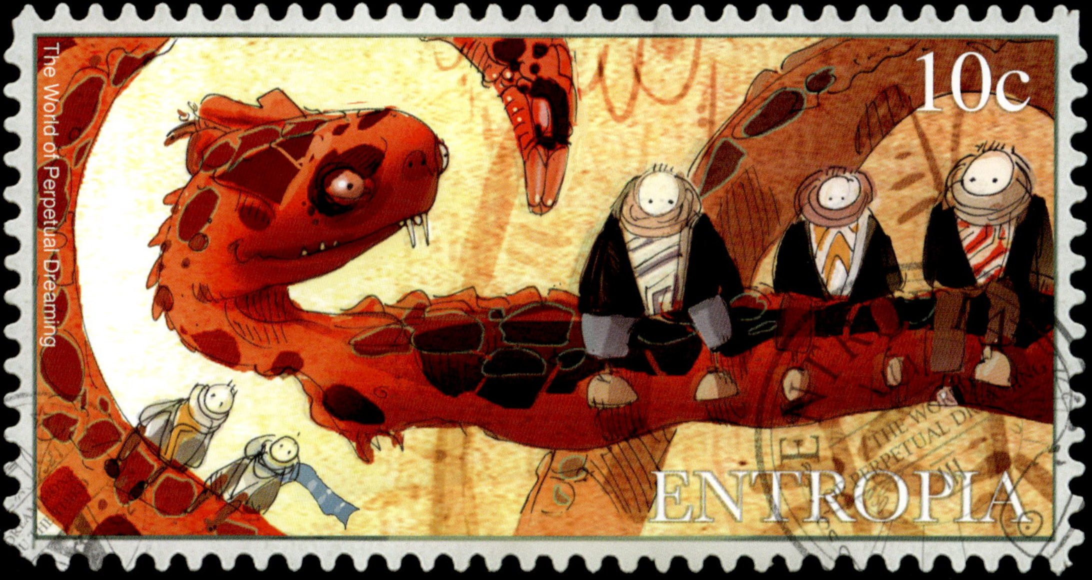

10c *The World of Perpetual Dreaming*

EDUCATIONAL STAMP

During wartime, the notorious Marquis de Salade fell in love with and married a middle-aged salad farmer named Mira Johnson.

His affection for Mira and her nine children was so great that he renounced all his land, which over time was turned into first-class salad fields, and his castle, which became the first orphanage for Entropia's war-children. His oldest daughter Toomba invented a brand of delicious salad dressing, which became so successful that it is now sold all over Entropia. All the profits from the Dressing du Marquis are used to build orphanages throughout the country and the de Salade family's generosity has become legendary. At age 65, his beloved wife died during the great influenza epidemic of lunar year 1033. Devastated, he started to consume large quantities of red naka nuts and was last seen wandering around aimlessly in the Fungus Sanctuary, wearing a limp salad wig.

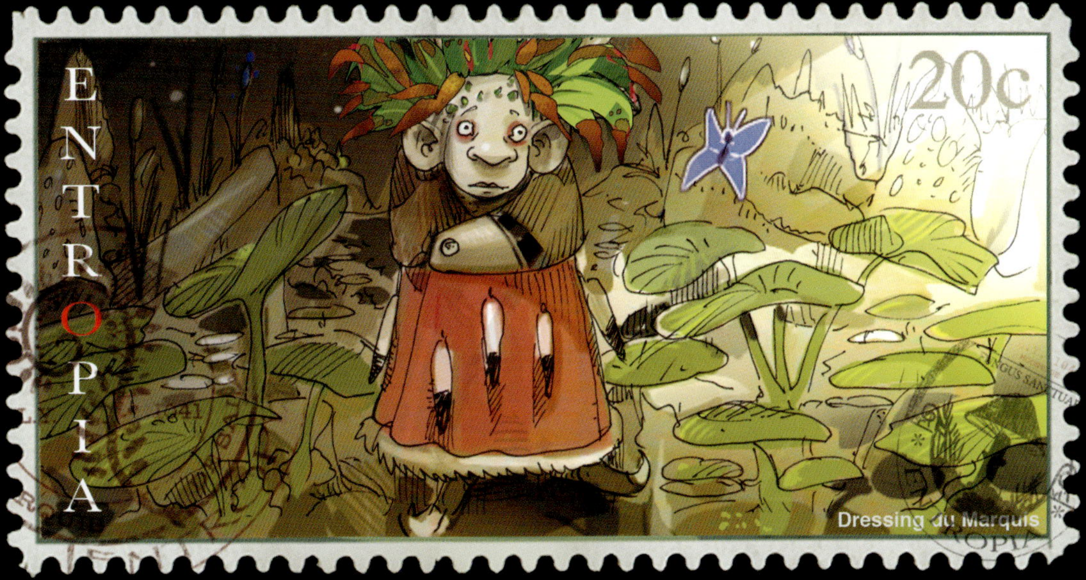

20c *Dressing du Marquis*

APPRECIATION STAMP

Two years after the end of the Oceanic Wars, a group of young archeologists discovered a series of copper-covered ziggurats hidden deep within Tukar's inaccessible mangrove forests. Since Tukar is notorious for dangerous lightning storms, the area has remained mostly unexplored.

The archeologists discovered a set of hieroglyphic symbols on the outside walls of the cone-shaped buildings that indicated the place had once been inhabited by an obscure group of weather druids, who had developed a mysterious cult involving lightning and storms. The discovery became even stranger when the archeologists entered the ziggurats and found three modern electrical generators marked with the seals of the Obsidian Brotherhood. It became apparent that here is where the fallen alchemists had tried for the first time to harness electrical power from lightning storms, a practice that was eventually perfected and used to power the monstrous Machine Cities of the Childish Robot Czar.

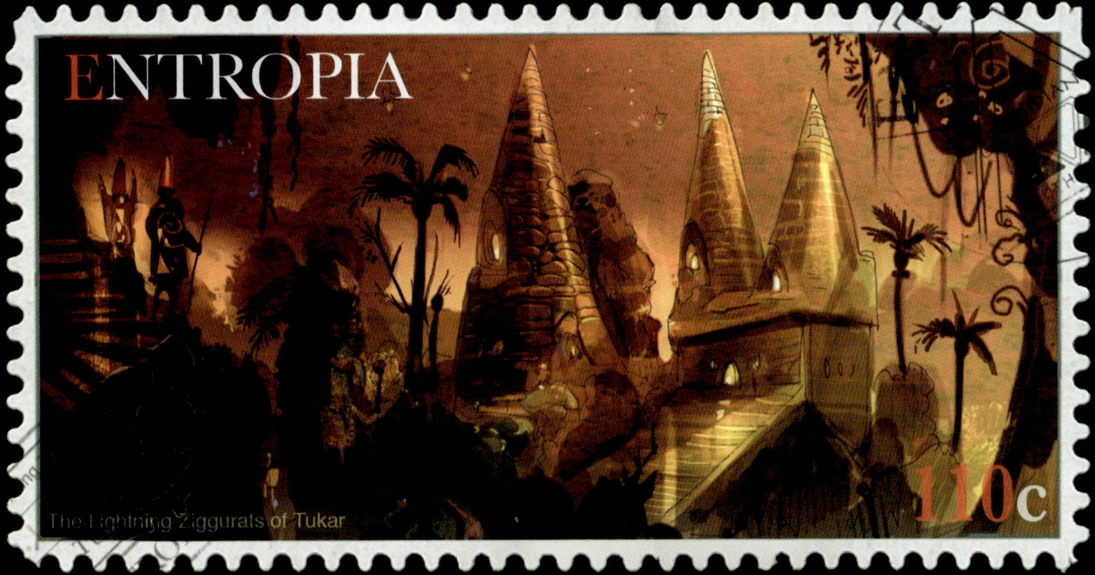

110c *The Lightning Ziggurats of Tukar*

HISTORICAL-CONSERVATION STAMP

Due to its proximity to the capital, Lake Rabbit Tooth is one of Entropia City's most favored recreation areas.

The center of the lake contains eight small beautiful islands that feature vacation cottages, camping and boating facilities, and even a miniature airstrip. On the biggest of the islands, an old villa has been converted into a lovely restaurant and a bed-and-breakfast inn.

Today, few tourists are aware that it was here where little Queen Pingo spent most of her childhood after the traumatic death of her parents. The bed-and-breakfast was her childhood home where she once lived with her aunt and uncle. The airstrip is where she first took off in her beloved airplane. On the smallest of the islands she retreated, sometimes for days, and played Scrabble with her pet goat Tinti.

Upon her return to the throne, Queen Pingo the Young turned Lake Rabbit Tooth over to Entropia's war-torn peoples, creating the first recreational nature preserve in Entropia.

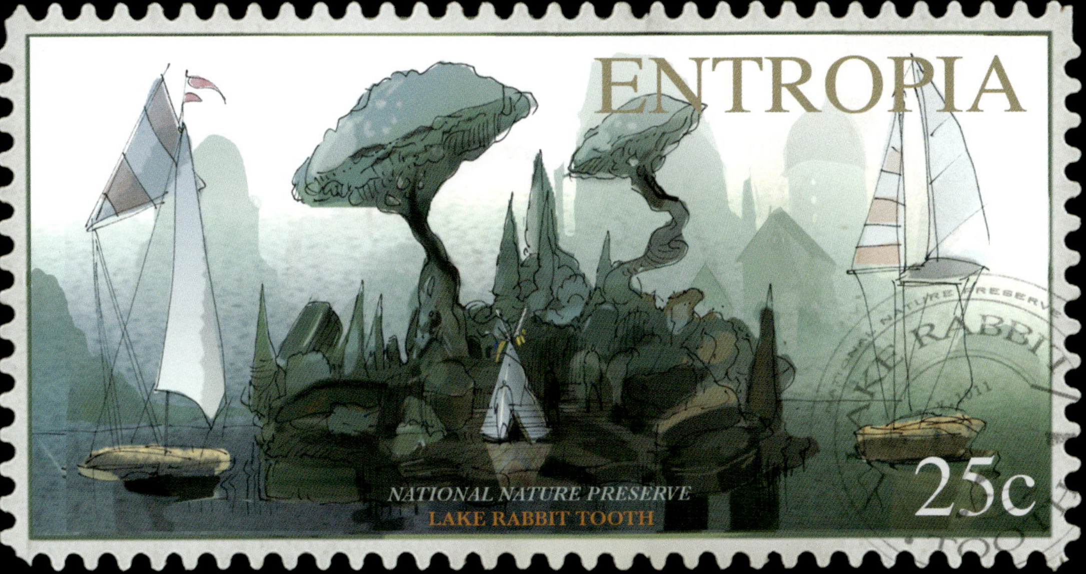

25c *Lake Rabbit Tooth*

NATURE-PRESERVATION STAMP

Sir Allen Mackenzie's bestselling diaries, ***Living Among the Akahui*** and ***Giant Turtles: Myth or Reality***, captured the imagination of all Entropians and made him a national hero. With his newly gained fame, he was able to finance bigger and more audacious expeditions year after year.

His final expedition led him south to the Ice Sanctuary of Diridamdam to film the elusive Horned Snow Devils. Regrettably, he made the fatal mistake of replacing his faithful sled dogs with a mechanized snow bicycle, sealing his doom. On his way back from Diridamdam, his snow-bike got stuck in the ice forest, 150 miles away from his base station, Camp Hope.

This is the final page of his expedition diary:

"Sick of exhaustion and weakened by frostbite, I set up camp. I fired off my last signal flare and secured the localization beacon to the tent. Oh, my dear wife, I am afraid this night may be my last. Trading my snow dogs with a snow-bicycle was a great mistake, even if the snow devils had great fun with it. My darling, I hope this diary will be found and the fantastic footage of the snow devils will not go to waste. It's getting dark and cold…I think I might step out and observe the giant icicles in front of my tent…they look beautiful in the moonlight…"

Sir Allen Mackenzie's empty tent was discovered two weeks later by a rescue expedition that came from Camp Hope. His body was never recovered. Some say he is still alive and wandering the region, documenting and filming his latest adventures.

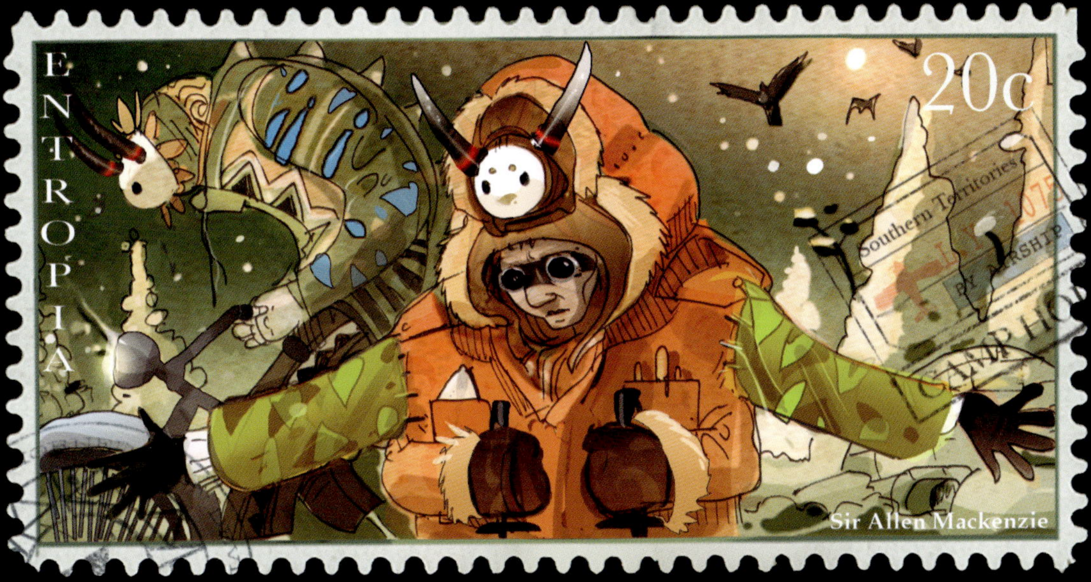

20c *Sir Allen Mackenzie's Last Expedition*

EXPLORATION STAMP

On the third moon tide of lunar year 1054, the distinguished university professor Nunzio Helium, also known as Nunzio the Boy Genius, rode on the 7:45 a.m. air rail from Entropia Station to his beloved university, as he had done for the last 39 years. During his long life, he had served as the Queen's flight instructor and confidant, designed airships and airplanes, invented safe balloon-cities, and engineered the acclaimed underwater-rail system. His favorite invention, however, was the public air-rail and its thousand bridges. On this particular trip, four minutes into the journey and while riding over the Zodiac Bridge, his heart stopped. He looked so peaceful, smiling at the sun with his eyes closed, that none of the passengers around him realized this was Nunzio's last ride.

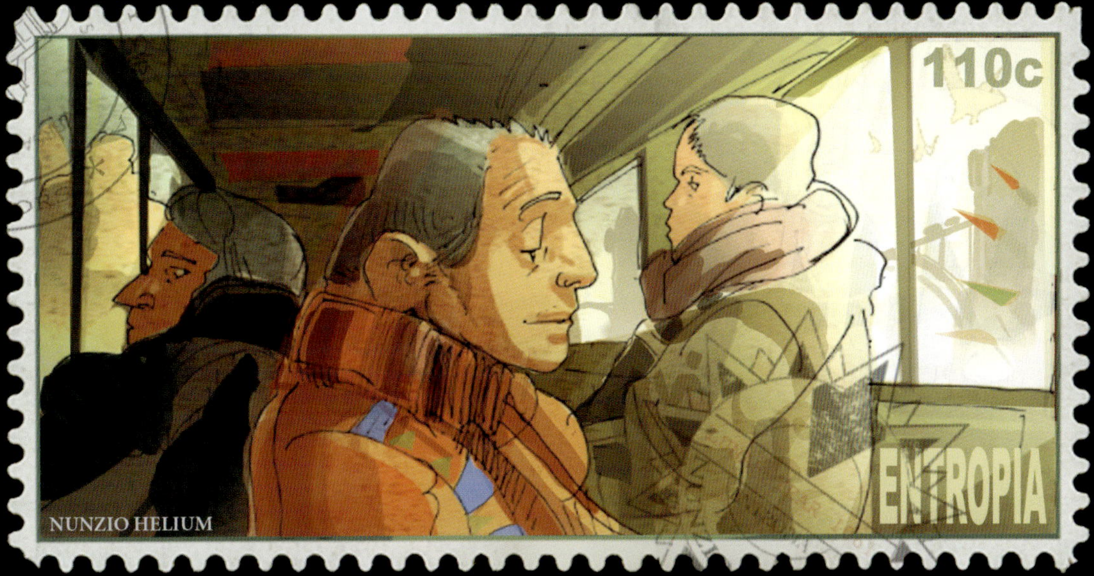

110C *Nunzio's Last Ride*

COMMEMORATIVE STAMP

During her old age, Genevieve Pongo, Queen Pingo's aunt and personal tutor, became good friends with the famous Artwark painter Andrew. They were frequently seen wandering through the parks of Entropia City or having tea in their favorite bistro on Lake Rabbit Tooth. Together they developed the first educational children's book series, ***How to Teach a Dinosaur to Read***. Aunt Pongo provided the text, while Andrew painted the beautiful and often eclectic illustrations. The book became an instant hit and is now found in every Entropian classroom.

In the following years, they created many more titles such as ***How to Teach a Dinosaur to Count***, ***How to Teach a Dinosaur to Sing***, and the lesser-known title, ***How to Teach a Dinosaur to Make a Macramé Owl***.

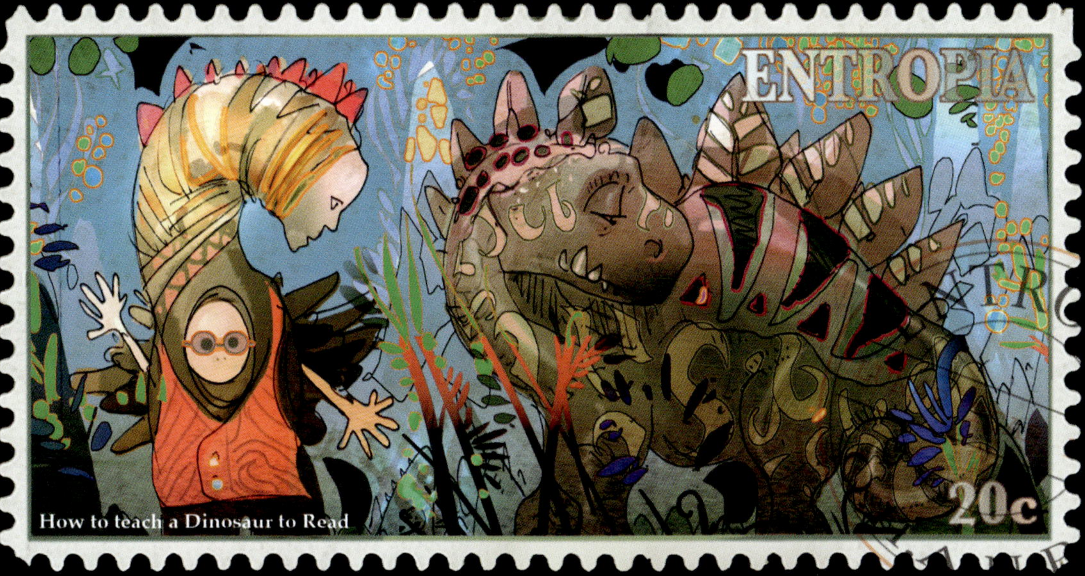

20c *How to Teach a Dinosaur to Read*

EDUCATIONAL STAMP

On her one hundred-and-fifth birthday, Queen Pingo, who always remained young at heart, died surrounded by her nine children, 14 grandchildren, and all of her friends and lovers. During her long life, she was able to unite the 15 provinces of Entropia and make peace among Entropians, Axolotls, and all sentient beings.

The news of Queen Pingo's death traveled like a shockwave throughout Entropia. When she was laid to rest in the Bay of Takashiro, mourners from all over Entropia attended her funeral. The naka farmers descended from the highlands and walked to the ocean shore, countless airships gathered over the bay, and thousands of Takashiro women in their kayaks escorted the funeral boat when it took to the sea for Queen Pingo's final journey.

It is documented that even the Wilderwhales emerged from the ocean to say farewell to a true daughter of Entropia.

Note: Despite her renouncement of the royal crown, for Entropia's sentient beings, Pingo would always remain their Queen.

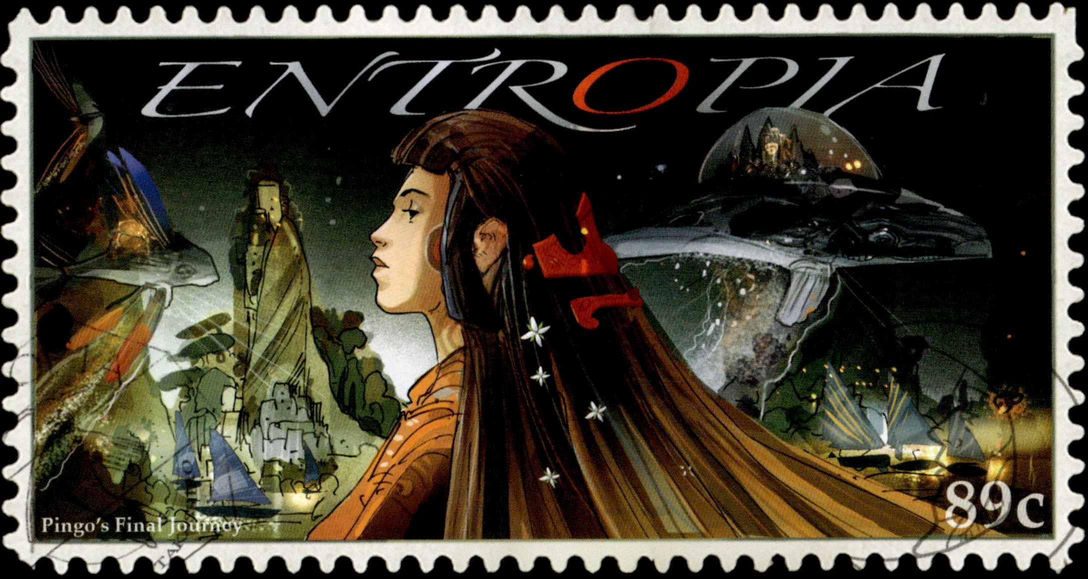

89c *Queen Pingo's Final Journey*

COMMEMORATIVE STAMP

ENTROPIA CITY OPERA
GRAND OPENING 75th ANNIVERSARY
THE TWO AND A HALF TENORS
ENTROPIA
LUNAR YEAR 1012
26th ANNUAL DESERT RACE OF THE SOUTHERN TERRITORIES
HELIUM IS FUN AND SAFE!
THE BIRKENWURST-CORNICHON
L.Y 911
PEACE BRIDGE
THE SECRET GUILD OF CROISSANT BAKERS
C.R.C
ENTROPIA
BY AIRSHIP
ENTROPIA
DRAGONFLY HUNTERS OF AKAHUI
EQUINOX
LUNAR YEAR 968
ENTROPIA
ROSE MONKS OF ST. ALBERTINO
ENTROPIA
KUKURSK
FIREWORKS FAIR
KUKURSK
THE GREAT UNDERWATER
LUNAR YEAR 935
TAKANU
ENTROPIA
L.V. 985
THE BATHING GIANTS
ENTROPIA
3
River Monuments
L.Y. 1121
BY AIRSHIP
ENTROPIA
Home of the
MINICOW
I.F.O.B. KANDINSK
ENTROPIA
KUKURSK
ENTROPIA
L.Y. 1002
ENTROPIA
KUNDUR
BANNED SINCE L.Y.1010
FRANCOISE DE CHANTILLY
DANCE TROUPE
EQUINOX
GORDONZOLA AND MARKUS
FANTASY FIRE SHOW
ENTROPIA
NAKA FARMERS OF TIKA